Why Aren't Christians More Like Jesus?

Michael J. Clemens

PUBLICATIONS

An Imprint of Sulis International Press
Los Angeles | Dallas | London

Cover photo by Stefan Kunze. Cover design by Sulis International Press.

ISBN (print): 978-1-958139-49-3
ISBN (eBook): 978-1-958139-50-9

Published by Keledei Publications
An Imprint of Sulis International
Los Angeles | Dallas | London

www.sulisinternational.com

Contents

Prologue 1

Introduction 5

1. Biblical Essentials 9

2. Twisting Scripture......................................23

3. From Constantine to Catholicism 41

4. Churchianity 57

5. Christianity 79

6. Loving God..89

7. Loving Others...113

8. More Like Jesus 131

9. The Great Omission 147

10. The Seduction of Partisan Politics........161

11. Following Jesus, No Matter What........181

Epilogue 193

Acknowledgements 195

About the Author...197

About the Publisher 199

Prologue

Do you wonder why many Christians are not more like Jesus? The fundamental reasons are simple, but the details of how and why that happened are complicated. Today, some settle for merely going to church where many of Christ's teachings are minimized or ignored. Rather than following God's son as their Lord and Master, such churchgoers view Jesus almost like an icon-mascot, a good guy who taught some good things.

Looking back through church history, this problem is not new. Apostolic practices (after Christ's crucifixion) emphasized a relationship with God and with others, but those traits greatly diminished after Constantine the Great. In the fourth century, Christianity became the official religion of the Roman Empire. While the development of creeds, clergy, and canon were helpful in many ways, in time they caused Christianity to turn away from its original focus. Instead of an emphasis on following Jesus, the religion bearing his name became more about church attendance and following a few rules, instead of following Christ. His church became "Christendom"—structured and hierarchical—like the Roman government. Being a member in good standing mattered most. Teachings on discipleship were given a back seat or ignored.

The Protestant Reformation, which began with Martin Luther in 1517, tried to address some of these problems, but largely failed. Over the following centuries, this broad attempt at reform lapsed back into the same organizational focus that emphasized belonging to the right church. Once again, the teachings of Jesus got lost. Being a Christian became a matter of mental assent to a belief system that did not carry through in practice like it had when the apostles acted on what Jesus commanded. Christianity became a matter of orthodoxy (right doctrine or belief) without a corresponding orthopraxy (right practice). Modern evangelicalism, for example, emphasizes making converts, but can fail to nurture those new believers into disciples who daily seek a Christlike life that goes beyond church membership and rule-keeping. Rather than being Christianity, much of today's institutional faith should be called "churchianity," because it largely leaves out Christ except as a ceremonial namesake.

For several reasons, many young adults still admire Jesus, but now want nothing to do with an organized religion that uses his name. While some churchgoers have left, others hang on, knowing something is not right, but not getting much help from their church or its leaders.

But there is hope in what I call "Jesus BC"—before churchianity, before Christendom, and before Constantine, Jesus said, "follow me." Today, we more often hear only about going to church. Why not both? God's son taught his followers how to live a life shaped by his example and teaching. Personal transformation, one moment at a time, in relationships with our heavenly father and with others, has always been at the heart of becoming more like Jesus. It can be so again.

This book first briefly surveys church history to explore these areas. Then I will suggest biblical answers for struggling believers and for church leaders interested in helping churchgoers become authentic disciples who try to follow Jesus more each day as best they can. This distinction will become important on Judgment Day when our heavenly father will welcome Christ-followers into eternal life, while mere churchgoers will find that they built their lives on sand (Matt 7:26).

Introduction

This book's title should resonate with most of Christianity, but the proposed solutions here arise from my background in Churches of Christ. Thus, these views may be more useful to those from evangelical traditions, not necessarily to all who consider themselves Christian.

My approach tries to help believers assess whether they are mere churchgoers or authentic Christ-followers. Those who depend on church leaders for guidance may not want to read this. But sincere believers who will individually face God on Judgment Day may find it revealing.

Why aren't Christians more like Jesus? That core question boils down to orthopraxy (right practice): what happens after conversion. Do most converts authentically try to follow and thus become more like Jesus? Or do they become mere churchgoers rather than embarking on a lifelong journey toward spiritual maturity? Such a concern is relevant to all of Christianity.

Hard questions require serious reflection; an emphasis on spiritual development might get lost amid efforts to reverse declining membership. My premise is that some religious leaders do not fully understand their basic purpose, to help each churchgoer develop into a Christ-follower.

All believers, regardless of sectarian identity, might find the following an acceptable, unifying aspiration. Unlike early creeds which focused on belief, the following proposal emphasizes total behavior.

EACH CHRISTIAN'S BEHAVIORAL GOAL

Each person who believes in Jesus of Nazareth as the Christ, the Messiah, should accept him as not just their Savior, but also as their Lord and Master. While some churchgoers want Jesus to save them from hell and deliver them to heaven, they reject his authority over how they live. The New Testament does not support such an approach as the following passages illustrate.

In the Gospels, Jesus called the twelve to "follow me" (John 1:43). He said that his sheep listen to his voice, and they "follow me" (John 10:27). Again, in John 12:26, Jesus says, "Whoever serves me must follow me..." In chapter 21 of John's gospel, the text repeats that mandate (to follow me) at the end of verses 19 and 22. Students should become like their teacher (Luke 6:40). The apostles Paul and Peter echo that message. Believers are to become "living sacrifices," not conformed to "this world," but transformed (Rom 12:1-2). We are to become holy, like Jesus (1 Pet 1:15-16), who left us an example to follow in his steps (1 Pet 2:21).

No believer, of course, will be able to perfectly follow Jesus who was sinless (1 Pet 2:22), but on Judgment Day, each believer will be graciously assessed. Did they know Jesus well enough to put his words into practice (Matt 7:24-27)? More importantly, did Jesus know them (Matt 7:23)?

God still calls everyone to become believers (2 Pet 3:1-9) and appeals to all to become his Son's disciples. But rather than just going to church, where their spiritual development may suffer, those who take their Saviour seriously should become authentic, lifelong, Christ-followers, becoming more like Jesus.

1.
Biblical Essentials

Unless you understand the Bible for yourself,
you are at the mercy of others.

In the late 1970's, I chaired the jury for a criminal trial. During our private deliberations, one of the jurors wanted to ask the court a question, so I passed along the message. After the note was relayed by the bailiff to the judge, he replied, "You already have all you need to render a verdict one way or the other." When it comes to responding to God, so do we. The Bible tells us enough to make our own decisions about Jesus of Nazareth (see John 20:31).

APPROACH

While different churches use the Bible differently, I focus on right practice (orthopraxy) rather than only right belief (orthodoxy). Both are important and connected, but this book emphasizes how Christians should live out their beliefs each moment of each day. Why this choice?

Right beliefs are essential for an unshakable foundation to build upon and should be the underlying motivation for each believer's daily faith-walk. But right belief by itself is useless. Jesus said that just calling him Lord was not enough. To "enter the kingdom of heaven," believers needed to do what he said (Matt 7:21-29). The followers of Christ are called to pursue God's agenda by their attitudes, words, and actions, not merely to hold certain beliefs. At the end of time, believers will be held accountable—not based upon a test of our beliefs, but based upon how we lived out God's ways. Early believers understood, and so should we, that faith is not about our perfection, but rather our direction—progress toward becoming more like Jesus.

This book takes the authority of the Bible seriously, but questions the ways that some theologians and church leaders have interpreted Scripture. Organizations tend to become bureaucratic over time; religion is no different. Church hierarchy often emphasizes their key doctrinal beliefs, but neglects to explore their institutional deficiencies. That is common for individuals, too. Who likes to focus on their own list of shortcomings? However, as a result, some of the plainest New Testament teachings can get lost. Teachings from Jesus should always be foremost if we are truly his disciples doing our best to follow him as Lord and Master, not just treat him as our Savior.

THE NEED FOR PERSONAL STUDY

One goal of this book is to encourage believers to study on their own, so that they can test the theology and practice of their leaders and teachers. The New Testament points out the need for personal study (2 Tim 2:15) and confirms that it was done (Acts 17:11). Jesus warned about "false prophets" (Matt 7:15) and cautioned against "rules taught by men" (Matt 15:9). Luke records Paul warning church elders that, "Even from among your number men will arise and distort the truth to draw away disciples after them" (Acts 20:30). Paul urged readers, "Do not go beyond what is written" (1 Cor 4:6). Jesus' earthly brother, James, wrote that those "who teach will be judged more strictly" (Jas 3:1). The apostle Peter wrote that interpretation requires diligence; concerning Paul's letters, he said that they:

> ...contain some things that are hard to understand, which ignorant and unstable people distort, as they do the other scriptures, to their destruction. Therefore, dear friends, since you already know this, be on your guard so that you may not be carried away by the error of lawless men... (2 Pet 3:16-17).

John says that believers should always test what they are taught, "...because many false prophets have gone out into the world" (1 John 4:1). Those warnings remain valid today.

Biblical interpretation on controversial topics can be especially difficult, but doing your best to let Scripture speak for itself is a defensible approach. Many of the commands, parables, and principles of Jesus contain simple, yet profound, theology. His points are easy to understand, but hard to put into practice. Memorizing key passages can provide a spiritual guide for daily life. What Jesus taught should be written on each believer's heart, in their mind, in their life.

Some churches and their leaders place more emphasis on proper beliefs than on proper practice. This is not surprising because the latter is difficult to gauge and requires apprenticeship by someone more mature to teach pathways to growth. Theologians publish volumes about various doctrines—but each believer's goal should be to study the Bible to learn: "How should I think, talk, and live?" Briefly, churchgoers tend to passively accept an emphasis on orthodoxy while Christ-followers actively pursue orthopraxy; a critical challenge is how to balance the two.

If the only teaching believers receive is from broad sermons, then their faith might not develop because their personal situation will often escape detailed consideration. Such cases require those in the pew to rely upon clergy. Giving someone a fish to feed them is helpful in the short term, but it also keeps them dependent. Those who teach others how to fish must grapple with each person's particular strengths and weaknesses, because everyone learns differently. However, once taught how to fish for themselves, churchgoers can move beyond basics in their spiritual lives and keep growing. There are many ways to learn biblical lessons besides listening to pulpit preaching and several of those additional methods of instruction can be very helpful.

SOLID INTERPRETATION (*EXEGESIS*)

The word *exegesis* (Greek: "to draw out") refers to the concentrated study of a passage to understand what it means. While Christian tradition accepts the Bible's authority, it is an understatement to say that interpretations vary. This is why it is essential to focus on its core teachings and why doing your own studying is critical. Some churchgoers are content to sit in pews and let their church leaders tell them what is important for a Christian's life. While this may be helpful for new believers who need basic orientation to the faith, at some point all of us must learn to explore Scripture for ourselves. Parents feed their young children and care for them. But to become independent adults, children must eventually learn how to think and do things on their own, a lifelong endeavor. In the same way, developing your own personal faith should be an ongoing process because spiritual growth often involves meeting challenges.

Not all Bible books can be understood in the same way. The Gospels and Acts are both selective narratives, making them easy to follow, like a story or a novel. The epistles of the New Testament are written like actual letters from that day, but those writing styles and formats are quite different from today's correspondence. Apocalyptic literature (Daniel, parts of Ezekiel, and most of Revelation) is a difficult genre to understand, and should be studied with extreme care.

Casual readers of the Bible may not understand the difference between descriptive narrative, stories that explain cultural realities, and normative guidance, godly instructions to believers. That ability alone will help those interested in following Jesus to grasp the difference between the times being discussed, and how believers should live their lives to become more like Jesus.

APPLIED INTERPRETATION

People often overlook their own shortcomings while judging others. New Testament teachings address this issue, directing that all believers should hold themselves accountable. There are two broad methods about how to do that. First, each Christian should practice self-discipline and introspection while at the same time extending grace to others. We should use Scripture as a mirror to examine ourselves (Jas 1:22 -25), not as a magnifying glass to criticize others (Matt 7:1-5). Always try to use the Bible's many messages to help reflect upon and overcome your own behavioral shortcomings—the person you are most able to change. Second, to help us see ourselves as others see us, we rely on relationships with our spiritual siblings in the faith, ministering to one another and holding each other accountable. These "one-another" verses (see Chapter 7, "Loving Others") require intimate, in-depth conversations with other believers.

None of the above is meant to suggest that leaders do not have an important role for they clearly do, and Scripture certainly provides for that. Further, they will be held to a higher standard (Matt 23:23, Jas 3:1) and rightly so. In many stages of their spiritual development, churchgoers depend greatly on their leaders, who thus bear substantial responsibilities. But since church leaders are also human, their teachings should still be examined in the light of Scripture. Unfortunately, church history contains many examples of religious leaders who led their followers astray.

LOST IN TRANSLATIONS?

Knowledge of the Bible's original languages (Hebrew, Greek, and Aramaic) is not necessary for Christian life, but a reasonable understanding of how languages work is helpful when studying Scripture. While many others around the world learn another language besides their mother tongue, most Americans do not, because English is an international language. But that also means that many in this country fail to realize the challenges of accurately translating ideas from one language to another, a lesson clear to those who know more than one language. As a result, many Americans do not realize the nuanced meanings behind many biblical passages.

Understanding the New Testament use of the word "love" can be challenging. Early Christians focused on radical love, which set them apart from the surrounding culture. This *agape* love, based upon God's love, is a deep, sacrificial love that places the well-being of others ahead of self. While there is some overlap between *agape* (sacrificial love) and *philia* (friendship love), their difference is contrasted by an exchange between Jesus and Peter in John 21:15-17. In English, we use one word for love, but it is often important to know which Greek word is being translated. Since love is such a key teaching, its different meanings require serious thought.

Translation issues arise from other words as well. The Greek word *baptizo* meant "to soak" or "to immerse." When translations from original languages began to appear, the transliterated word "baptize" (borrowed directly from the Greek) had already become part of church terminology and practice—which was sprinkling. This has resulted in debates about the difference between immersion and sprinkling, as well as the practice of infant baptism (by sprinkling), which became popular after Christianity became the official religion of the Roman Empire. Thus, while the concept is not found in Scripture, the practice of sprinkling had been established by tradition. Rather than translate these words literally, which could have caused a problem for the institutional church, they simply transliterated the Greek word into "baptize" or "baptism."

As your primary Bible for personal study, find a modern translation developed from the original languages by a committee of scholars. Besides rigorous translations, paraphrased versions can help communicate the meaning of many passages. *The Living Bible* (Kenneth N. Taylor), and *The Message* (Eugene H. Peterson) use modern language to make Scripture easier to understand.

Once you have a reliable, modern, and readable translation, and others for comparison, consider obtaining at least one reference book on how to study the Bible. One of the best is *How to Read the Bible for All Its Worth* by Gordon D. Fee and Douglas Stuart. Gradually build up your own reference works so you will have reliable tools to help you grapple with controversial passages. Software Bibles often contain various versions among their search features. For those who prefer the King James Version, I recommend *The Word, The Bible from 26 Translations*, edited by Curtis Vaughan. Its verse-by-verse text lists alternate wording from King James English which thus makes for convenient comparisons to illustrate shades of meaning, not otherwise obvious.

Besides its difficult readability, I do not recommend the King James Version (KJV) because of its archaic language. For example, its translation of 1 Thessalonians 5:22 reads "Abstain from all appearance of evil," while the 1973 New International Version reads "Avoid every kind of evil." That contrast in meanings can make quite a difference when you try to put the phrase into action. Sermons based on the KJV version would say that Christians would need to avoid even looking like you are doing something bad, whereas the NIV (closer to the Greek text) suggests that avoiding evil is what matters, not how things look. Otherwise, Jesus could not have met with sinners or interacted with known prostitutes. Since Christ associated with such social outcasts, it does not make sense that the above verse meant that we should never associate with those who are not believers. This illustrates the misunderstanding of just one text; there are many others.

CONTEXT MATTERS

Context is crucial to understanding the Bible which is not a topical reference book where you can look up, in one place, all references to a particular subject. Scripture includes various narratives and genres. Its meanings depend on many factors including: cultural setting, linguistic usage, literary flow, specific history, and more. While the Greek and Roman cultures were somewhat like modern Western cultures, the Hebrew Bible was written in the Ancient Near East, a culture which is quite different, and sometimes baffling to American believers. Understanding cultural context will help readers comprehend any biblical message to its contemporary audience. It has been said that a biblical passage cannot mean now what it did not mean when it was written.

Some biblical concepts describe the culture of their time, but are not required by the Christian faith. Such things have more to do with social realities rather than faith issues. For example, several passages in the New Testament discuss the role of faith for masters and slaves. Sadly, throughout history, some have used this to support the institution of slavery. Historians tell us that the Roman Empire contained millions of slaves, so the government always feared an uprising. Thus, to speak out against slavery was considered sedition. That was the reality for writers of the New Testament, but does not mean they either condoned slavery or preached rebellion against Rome—they were simply writing about their culture. Still, some passages do speak against enslaving others (1 Tim 1:10 condemned "slave traders" [NIV] or "men-stealers" [KJV]; see also Paul's letter to Philemon). Prior to America's Civil War, these passages were ignored by church leaders who misused the Bible to support a slave-based agrarian economy. To be fair, some abolitionists who wanted to end slavery also based views on their religious beliefs.

Despite our need for understanding cultural context, my main point remains: most of the commands of Jesus and his teachings to followers are straightforward. "Love your enemies" might be done in different ways by different people in different cultures, but the principle remains relatively easy to comprehend. However, putting it into practice will be much more challenging regardless of cultural context—a key difference between orthodoxy and orthopraxy. Believing something does not mean that it can easily be put into practice. While I might believe I should demonstrate Peter's building blocks of faith (2 Pet 1:5-8), authentically practicing each one is much more difficult. That is why a believer's life should be a process of continual growth.

FIRST IMPRESSIONS CAN LAST

Many children have been taught various Bible doctrines at young ages. Without age-appropriate clarifications as they get older, they may retain a childlike view of God. Any toxic teachings from youth can impact one's view of God as a heavenly cop just waiting to catch someone in sin. Some authors, for example, put into print that their conversion from unbeliever to churchgoer was prompted by a fear of going into hell's fire for eternity. Without the benefits of ongoing study, some adult churchgoers still carry in their mind similar religious baggage from their youth.

MOVING FORWARD

While relying on more mature Christians and church leaders for nurture and guidance, we each still need to work on our own by studying Scripture with help from authoritative references. After all, Jesus said, "You are my friends if you do what I command" (John 15:14). How can believers obediently respond if they do not know his commands and what they mean in practice?

Like many things, learning to correctly balance our belief with practice will always be personal. It is also important for each new believer to understand the basics of their faith—what to believe and how to live it out—before trying to teach others. Some churches with new converts begin immediately encouraging them to go out and evangelize others, without properly preparing them to develop their own faith. Such practices illustrate one conflict between the institutional goal of gaining members versus the individual, but personal, lifelong goal of becoming Christlike. It can be devastating to an immature believer to try to convert an unbeliever who raises questions that cannot be answered by someone who has not learned even the basics of their Christian faith.

Self-study is important—not only to help ourselves mature, but also to test what we are being taught by others as Scripture encourages us to do. Even theologians and leaders can be wrong.

2.
Twisting Scripture

*The Bible is often misused, so it is helpful to
learn how to recognize some common abuses.*

Have you ever wondered why the Bible gets interpreted to claim that God says so many different
things about what Christians are supposed to think
or do? With several high-profile religious groups
being politically active based upon their church
doctrine or understanding of Scripture, biblical interpretation has been elevated to a matter of public
discussion.   But even among those who share a
high regards for Scripture's adequacy, differences
will always be with us. Still, when reasonable people disagree on interpretation, a workable vocabu-
lary, terms, and language should allow us to clarify
the issues involved so that at least we can agree on
what we disagree about.

Besides, the New Testament's inspired books do
not answer all possible questions. How do those
doing their best to follow Christ make sense of his
parables packed with layers of meaning? How do
his followers digest challenging passages to develop a clear understanding about practicing their
faith? My answer is "seriously and with care." That

is why personal study is essential. But part of serious interpretation includes becoming familiar with some predictable problem areas.

To start, this book assumes familiarity with biblical content and its teachings about Jesus. If you have not read much of your Bible, especially the New Testament, it is a mistake to read it just to find what you already believe. Such an approach is called confirmation bias. It is much more helpful, though difficult for some, to read Scripture simply to gain an understanding of its basic messages, especially those that are repeated (indicating they are more important). Taking a fresh look at Scripture, maybe in a different translation, should make you more open to evaluating your own long-held views probably inherited from parents, friends, or church. If nothing else, rereading the Gospels, which tell the same story in different ways, will help you gauge the range of teachings personally delivered by the one claiming to be God's son. By studying his parables, especially those explained in the text, you will have a good start to becoming more like Jesus.

SOME PARTS OF THE BIBLE ARE MORE IMPORTANT THAN OTHERS

Christianity is unquestionably grounded in the writings of the Hebrew Bible (Old Testament). Jesus often quotes these scriptures. All the writers of the New Testament rely upon the imagery, theology, and understanding of God from the Old Testament. Jesus spoke mainly to Jews during his lifetime. Much of the early church was made up of Jewish converts. Some say that you cannot truly understand the teachings of the New without a good understanding of the Old (see, for example, Rom 15:4 or Gal 3:24). But this does not mean that all teachings of the Hebrew Bible still hold the same meaning today for Christians that they do for Jews.

The death, burial, and resurrection of Jesus presented a new covenant that was foretold in the Old Testament (see Jer 31:31-34) and affirmed in the New (see 2 Cor 3:6; Heb 8:8-13, 9:15-28). While basic beliefs (theology, ethics, and morals) are similar, some practices differ. Briefly, love fulfills the law (Rom 13:8-10). Believers could spend endless hours studying the history, culture, and teachings of the Old Testament. While it is helpful for a Christian to understand differences between the covenants, following Jesus means paying the most attention to his teachings.

Some translations place the words of God's son in red print. These are often called "red-letter" editions or "red-letter Bibles." Directly attributed to Jesus, such passages almost always contain essential and needful elements of Christian faith and practice. Because they came from one who spoke with authority, unlike the scribes, his words are worthy of any believer's closest attention.

What Jesus called the two Greatest Commandments remains a major way that the new covenant reflects the old covenant. The first four commandments of the decalogue focus on relationships with God; the last six tell how we should treat others. While Jesus affirmed the two Greatest Commandments, he went beyond the Golden Rule (Matt 7:12) and said that we should love our enemies (Matt 5:44). In the Sermon on the Mount, Jesus describes the proper attitudes, words, and actions for his followers—a new law, so to speak, that goes further than the Law of Moses.

Overcome with wonder at the sight of Jesus, Moses, and Elijah during the Transfiguration, Peter wanted to build three shelters or tabernacles, one for each. But a voice from heaven said, "This is my Son, whom I love; with him I am well pleased. Listen to him" (Matt 17:5). That is still true.

The apostle Paul calls Jesus the "one mediator between God and man, the man Christ Jesus" (1 Tim 5:7). On Judgment Day, his words will be used to determine whether his believers took them to heart and put them "into practice" (Matt 7:21-29). Jesus also said, "I am the way and the truth and the life. No one comes to the Father except through me" (John 14:6).

Some believers like to focus mainly on Old Testament lessons. Others give passages from New Testament writers greater significance than messages from Jesus. Both approaches to Scripture need to consider the preeminence of what Christ said, and not treat other passages independently.

WORSHIPING THE BIBLE INSTEAD OF THE GOD IT REVEALS

Idolatry, the adoration or deification of something other than God, is condemned throughout the Hebrew Bible and the New Testament. That makes it especially ironic when some believers think and act as if the Bible itself, its printed words or even the physical book, is the center of their faith. This amounts to bibliolatry: treating the book as sacred instead of its message. Jesus warns about those who "diligently study the Scriptures" to possess "eternal life," but who then refuse to come to the one who offers them that life (John 5:39–40). God alone should be worshiped and Christians need to understand that the Son of Man represents God in the flesh (John 14:9).

The Bible is a means to an end, not an end in itself. Its written messages provide guidance about how to live, but its 31,000 plus verses cannot contain all of God's knowledge or thoughts. Thus, it cannot answer every question because that is not its purpose. What it does contain is enough for believers to know how to think, talk, and live as followers of Jesus. Still, dealing with the sacred can challenge anyone. Ancient Jews would not even pronounce the word "God" because they feared it would be too easy to not give the name above all names its proper respect. In contrast, the New Testament suggests that as believers, as children of God, we can say, "Abba, Father" (Rom 8:15-16).

This important difference between covenantal peoples suggests that Christians need to develop an intimacy with their heavenly father, whereas God would have seemed to remain more aloof to those whose temple worship clearly separated clergy and laity.

Giving the printed words of God more importance than authentically responding to those words from our heavenly father takes many forms. Examples of this type of misplaced emphasis can be seen in past use of Latin by the Vatican, or the King James Version (KJV) by Protestants. Church leaders acted as if only these translations were sacred so that only they could be relied upon for knowledge about God. Yet, even these translations, from earlier texts, required interpretation.

The Protestant Reformation helped make the Bible more accessible as more translations emerged. Especially late in the 20th century, after more readable translations were available besides the KJV, some Protestant churches religiously held on to the authorized version of 1611. Since the English language had changed in almost 400 years, its outdated expressions became difficult to understand, and contained words and phrases that sometimes had different (or even opposite!) meanings from current meaning and usage. While some liked King James English, others condemned supporters of newer versions because traditional words were being discarded. What caused this opposition? The language, not its meaning, had become sacred (bibliolatry), so to change any part of it was to challenge its authenticity, its validity, and its role as God's word.

Today's use of the King James Version has greatly declined in favor of modern translations. The Gideons, for example, moved away from the KJV in their widespread distribution of Bibles to hotel and motel rooms. But increased use of modern translations did not keep the concept of bibliolatry from finding new paths, however indirect those diversions may seem.

Defending the word of God from criticism can become an indirect type of bibliolatry when it fails to emphasize what Jesus says is important: doing what he said (Matt 7:26). While it is appropriate to defend the Bible from those who attack its meaning, circling the theological wagons against critics does not remedy the basic internal problem with modern Christianity: the major gap between what churches say they believe and how churchgoers actually behave.

An intense focus on orthodoxy (what you must believe) by a church relegates orthopraxy (how you should live) to secondary importance. To preserve their distinctive doctrine, many churches defend their theological turf, but institutions do not answer to God at Judgment—individuals do. Beliefs matter, but faith-filled living matters more. People who call him Lord, but do not respond to his words and "put them into practice" will not have a friend in Jesus (Matt 7:21-23, 26-27).

Rather than only debating or discussing right doctrine, churches should more strongly emphasize right practice, which must become each believer's priority. Helping struggling believers learn to follow Jesus by doing God's will must be done on a case-by-case basis. Broad-brush sermons have obvious instructional value, but often lack specific responses to each individual situation.

The main problem of human response to the messages from Christ is not a poor understanding of some finer points of obscure doctrine, or various types of biblical criticism. The core issue is a lack of focus on basic teachings that are easy to understand, but hard to live out. Thus, spiritual maturity requires an ongoing focus, keeping your eyes on Jesus. Without such a lifelong faith-goal, believers fall prey to Satan's pressures to ignore, minimize, or overlook what Jesus said. It is a problem if churchgoers say they believe in God, but still give Satan a foothold (Eph 4:27).

FLAWED INTERPRETATION (*EISEGESIS*)

Explained in the last chapter, *exegesis* means comprehensively studying a biblical text to draw out its intended original meaning. The opposite is called *eisegesis*—reading a predetermined meaning into the text. *Eisegesis* often tries to pretend to be *exegesis*, especially to support a view that is key to sectarian identity. Questionable teachings can also come from those who "do not know what they are talking about or what they so confidently affirm" (1 Tim 1:5-7).

Having a high regard for Scripture remains important to those who consider Jesus as Lord and Master, but taking his teachings seriously requires that they be understood. Some with a lesser regard for Scripture reinterpret its content to align with their personal views. It is always okay to review tradition to see if a particular teaching withstands scrutiny, but it is not okay to revise interpretation to suit customer-oriented religion as seems to be the case sometimes today.

Eisegesis occurs more often than we might think. Sectarian handcuffs sometimes limit what academics are allowed to formally conclude. For example, Vatican scholars must grapple with one verse (1 Cor 9:5) that allows the apostles, including Cephas (another name for Peter), to take along a believing wife. That speaks against celibacy (Matt 8:14 refers to Peter's mother-in-law).

Sometimes theologians fail to clarify the critical difference between direct teaching and indirect inferences about what scholars think God meant. Can we presume that God knew how to be clear about what was most important? Yes! When Scripture repeats a message or emphasizes it in other ways, what are we to conclude? For example, *agape* love must be a core teaching.

While we can all come to some creative interpretations of Scripture that we ourselves act upon in good conscience, there is a threshold of legitimacy that must be crossed before we teach others to accept our views on controversial issues. Matters of individual conscience, of course, do not always make sense to others, but must still be respected because "everything that does not come from faith is sin" (Rom 14:23b). Just as we should continually mature in our practice, it is also an ongoing issue to reaffirm and fine-tune our core beliefs about the nature of God. Just because those who follow Christ must emphasize orthopraxy does not mean they ignore orthodoxy. All believers should always strive for spiritual balance as they mature, not an easy challenge.

Proof Texting & Cherry Picking

Many who read the Bible are not aware of the historical changes that were made in the format of its text. Centuries passed before Scripture was divided into chapters and verses. Such indexing makes it easy to locate or reference specific passages, but it also allows for verses to be taken from their context and misused to make a preconceived point. We call this "proof texting." If a reader does not carefully consider the historical and cultural settings of a passage, its significance can be easily misunderstood. By disregarding its settings, passages can be misused to support whatever interpretations are being rationalized. It takes effort to understand the correct meaning of a passage in the context of surrounding verses and other verses elsewhere on the same subject.

Another flawed method of interpretation is cherry-picking which involves choosing only certain verses to support a particular view while ignoring passages that suggest alternative perspectives.

THE LEGACY OF ANTI-SEMITISM

Among the worst examples of proof texting and cherry picking are the biblical interpretations that promoted prejudice against all Jews as "Christkillers," a characterization reflected in one stand-up comedian's more famous routines. Fortunately, churches sometimes repent for flawed teachings and policies. Vatican II (1962-1965) apologized for its past depiction and treatment of Jews. Cultivating an institutional policy that promotes religious hate clearly conflicts with Christ's individual mandate to love. While the Vatican's apology was helpful, many generations accepted past policy as truth. Broad remedies take time to permeate culture, so anti-Semitism persists. To become more like Jesus, believers must adopt Christ-like values, which remain as countercultural today as when they were when first proclaimed and taught.

To recap, the past teaching and spread of anti-Semitism stems from the prejudicial narrative that the Jewish people killed Jesus. In fact, the New

Testament clearly documents (Matt 12:14, 26:4; Luke 22:2; John 11:53) that it was his own Jewish religious leaders who set up Jesus for execution because they considered him, as a Jew, to be a threat to their power and teachings. Not even all Jewish leaders were opposed to him, Nicodemus being a prime example. Jesus had many followers during his life, and they were almost exclusively Jews. The Twelve were Jewish. The use of one verse (Matt 27:25) to justify hatred ignores other verses that explain why Jesus was targeted. Those who wanted him killed could easily have paid for agents to agitate the crowd, just like the chief priests and elders made sure that the crowd wanted Barabbas spared instead of Jesus (Matt 27:20). Besides atonement theology, more could be said on this topic.

Anti-Semitism is unchristian. Sadly, its past teaching by churchianity has historically led extremist groups to rationalize their hatred of Jews. That is an inhumane, ungodly legacy.

GRACE VS. WORKS

One of Christianity's oldest doctrinal disputes is the "grace versus works" debate. Martin Luther, for example, considered the book of James to be "an epistle of straw." Luther apparently did not like this early letter's major emphasis on the practice of one's faith over and above the theology behind it. Taken to extremes, of course, those who focus on works tend toward legalism, a reversion to the old law. But those who focus on grace, as if "the obedience of faith" (Rom 1:5, 16:26, NASB) does not matter to God, ignore accountabilities. Both teachings warrant further study. Here some highlights:

In a remarkably clear theological summary, the apostle Paul said,

> … it is by grace you have been saved, through faith — and this not from yourselves, it is the gift of God— not by works, so that no one can boast. (Eph 2:8-9)

It is God who saves, so believers cannot legalistically work their way to heaven. But Paul then makes an important and relevant counterpoint about a disciple's response to divine salvation:

> For we are God's workmanship, created in Christ Jesus to do good works, which God prepared in advance for us to do. (Eph 2:10)

Even with correct beliefs and practice, our nature as imperfect human beings necessarily means that we cannot redeem ourselves. However, once you are saved, the proper response is gratitude toward God, which shows itself in good works. Such works do not save—they are the response to being saved. We are not saved by being good, we are good because we have been saved.

CHEAPENED GRACE

Those who consider themselves covered by God's grace because they belong to the right church, but do little in response to the teachings of Jesus, have cheapened God's grace. Why? They are violating the spirit of Romans 6:1, which argues against sinning to increase grace. While most churches teach against overt sin (several lists in the epistles give examples), how many teach about the sins of omission? That sin results from not doing the good that you know you should do (my paraphrase of Jas 4:17). Combining these two concepts (limiting discipleship to just avoiding certain sins while not doing the good that they should) amounts to a shortcut to keep a churchgoer "in good standing." Such a practice has been called "the law of least effort" in other areas of life, such as someone doing the least amount needed to pass a high school class so that they can play sports or keep an after-school job. Doing just enough to get by will not please God.

In contrast, earnest students learn as much as they can in each course, while serious employees do their best at their jobs. More to the point of what Jesus taught, those who "hunger and thirst for righteousness" will be filled (Matt 5:6). Those who reduce Christianity to surface level conversion and religious rule-keeping have missed the concepts of purpose beyond self, of sacrificial commitment, and of taking up one's own cross (Matt 10:38).

They might be fooling themselves into thinking that they are Christians when they might be mere churchgoers. Such church members may come to believe that their presence at religious gatherings validates their status before God instead of having to authentically practice what Jesus said (Matt 7:24-29).

How does the concept of cheapened grace creep into Christianity? If churches do not receive enough money to keep their doors open, they may have to close as several have had to do. Thus, churches become dependent on giving to survive, and can end up catering to their largest givers. Lessons based on it being "harder for a camel to go through the eye of a needle than a rich man to enter heaven" might not go over well in some circles (Matt 19:24; Mark 10:25; Luke 18:25).

Since today's churches need to attract more members, harsh but biblical messages that call for sacrifice and personal accountability tend to be minimized. Subtle changes like these can happen slowly over time, almost without being noticed, but are no less damaging than outright false teachings because they change the nature of the church from God-directed to consumer-oriented.

SPECIAL TRANSLATIONS

Bibles with a niche emphasis have appeared, clouding more basic messages. Some emphasize views such as end times or rapture theology, the prosperity gospel, trying to impose modern science onto creation narratives, and more. Making relatively narrow interpretations a primary focus is a mistake because that distracts from the core meaning of Christianity. Some versions subtly incorporate sectarian interpretations. The New World Translation emphasizes the doctrinal stances of Jehovah's Witnesses, the Scofield Bible emphasizes end times theology, and Catholic Bibles contain the Apocrypha.

MOVING FORWARD

Sadly, some churches have adopted an exceptionalist mindset: "We are correct, and if you disagree, you are wrong." The lack of openness to new ideas, different interpretations, and new understandings (based on solid study, not *eisegesis*) is a dangerous road for both Christian individuals and institutions, but is an all-too-common attitude. As people get older, and especially if they have been in a particular religious group for an extended time, they are less willing to even consider departure from church traditions that they view as infallible. Why do they think that they have learned all there is to know about God? Maybe because that is what they have been told. Chances are that their view of Christianity revolves around a doctrinal emphasis rather than on authentically practicing what Jesus taught. Christ's multi-layered, open-ended concept of discipleship remains something that can never be fully mastered. Even the most dedicated will still fall short of God's spiritual goals. What is left for those who focus mostly on their church doctrine? They often redouble their efforts to defend against any perceived criticism.

Mature spiritual leaders seek to draw out God's intended meaning from Scripture, rather than impose their own views onto it. It is okay to be unsure about the meaning of an obscure passage and even admit what remains unclear from among possible understandings. But the key issue is how to prioritize a sincere search of Scripture to determine what is involved in following Jesus.

Some churches emphasize Jesus as Savior, but then downplay Christ as Lord and Master. Such traditions stress the holiness of Jesus while de-emphasizing the more difficult parts of the faith that require personal sacrifice. Those who approach the need for spiritual discipline later, after a convert has become part of their church, employ bait-and-switch, a manipulative tactic. Why teach that a savior who sacrificed himself will require anything less from his followers?

For some church leaders who do not accept the ongoing responsibility of teaching their followers to become more like Jesus, it is easy to meander into peripheral questions. Several religious topics have little to do with a believer's faith or questions about how to live a life honoring Jesus.

In my high school English literature class, we would speculate about what long dead authors meant. While we can guess about the intent of writers who have passed away, our God will meet us at Judgment to explore our response to his words. When we stand before the only righteous judge at the end of time, when we throw ourselves on the mercy of that final court, will we be able to say that we have not gone off on doctrinal tangents? As you might suspect from the frequent repetition of this book's main theme, those who would claim Christ as God's son and their Savior would do well to listen to Jesus, our Lord and Master, who said, "Follow me."

3.
From Constantine to Catholicism

Those willing to examine the past can benefit from lessons learned by 20/20 hindsight.

In a family with several children, the younger ones eventually realize that, before they were born, the life of the family had been going on for years. They were not present in earlier family photos because they were not yet alive. Their later memories distort a full view of their family's history because they were not around to experience or observe it. Sometimes religious leaders and their followers are also unaware how religion, based upon the biblical Jesus, changed over time. Just as Scripture needs to be discussed in context, so does the history of modern Christianity.

Revisiting history does not mean it should be revised to make it more palatable to current sensitivities. Rather, looking back to the past is important for understanding where we have been. Many aspects of the past might seem particularly ugly or unpleasant, but must be accurately understood in the context of that time and culture. Just as today's cross-cultural understanding needs to be improved, so does our recognition of the dramatically different societal realities of the past.

SUMMARIZING THE CONSTANTINIAN SHIFT

Constantine the Great, the fourth century Roman Emperor, had a major impact on the Christian religion. Prior to his reign, Christianity was illegal and persecuted, but it then became the official religion of the Roman Empire. It is difficult to exaggerate the significance of this Constantinian shift as a relatively new religion moved from persecution to privileged status. Earlier converts to Christ risked their lives; in contrast, those who joined the church after its governmental acceptance faced no such trials. Before the Constantinian shift, Christians could be killed for their belief; later, those who did not convert could be killed for their unbelief.

It is not fair, of course, to attribute all of Christianity's post-apostolic changes to just one Roman emperor, but having one name to credit (or blame) makes a historical overview much easier. Those interested in pursuing detailed developments have many resources at their disposal.

FROM SPIRITUAL MOVEMENT TO RELIGIOUS INSTITUTION

Before Christianity became the official religion of the Roman Empire, followers in church communities focused upon becoming more like Jesus. Like

Judaism's adherents who memorized their Hebrew Bible, followed their rabbis, and tried to live out their beliefs, early Christians did something similar. They told stories about Jesus, they repeated his teachings, and they committed to memory key parts of what we now call Scripture. Their faith involved personal transformation within an intimate spiritual community. But after the Constantinian shift, Christianity became a structured institution with creeds, clergy, and canon (what became the New Testament). Gradual transition to the state church changed the character of what had been apostolic practice.

Though the Roman Empire vanished long ago, its influence remains. Early Christians tried to follow Jesus in thought, word, and deed. Modern Christianity has often lost that apostolic focus. In theological terms, early believers generally focused on orthopraxy (right practice) as an outcome of orthodoxy (right belief). After the Constantinian shift, this new religion's organizational focus shifted from personal deeds to gatekeeper creeds along with other systematized rituals.

WHY THE SHIFT FROM DEEDS (ORTHOPRAXY) TO CREEDS (ORTHODOXY)

The contrasting terms "deeds" and "creeds" oversimplify these concepts. Practice means more than what people do (their deeds) and belief means more than doctrinal summaries (their creeds). But before the Constantinian shift, the authentic practice of Christianity was expected from all believers (deeds). There was a strong emphasis on actions that accompanied such faith. Since they ran the risk of persecution and perhaps even imprisonment or death—no one was going to profess belief in Jesus as the Christ unless they lived it out in their daily lives. But with Christianity's acceptance by Rome, there was no longer any fear of persecution.

The new acceptability of being Christian made it easy to profess belief without the resulting life changes that the early Christians saw as essential to a living faith. If you said the right things (creeds) and did the basic requirements (church attendance, for example), a change in life (deeds) was not necessary because there were no consequences if you did not live your faith. If you professed belief in the official religion and publicly demonstrated the minimum requirements, you could live privately however you wished. Going to church replaced following Jesus.

This approach to being Christian has largely survived. Instead of practicing their faith daily by thoughts, words, and deeds, today's believers are now said to practice their faith if they attend religious services where they affirm creeds, key doctrines, or statements of faith. Such a change from the practices of apostolic Christianity is difficult to grasp without carefully looking back.

CREEDS HAD VALUE

In earliest Christianity, word of mouth was the primary manner used to spread and teach faith. Basic statements of belief, more commonly known as creeds, originally served several purposes. When the Apostles' Creed or Nicene Creed were recited during worship, for example, they helped church-goers remember basic theology in a predominantly oral culture. They also helped distinguish between core beliefs and doctrinal variations seen as heresy or unorthodox teachings.

While most early creeds were based on sound theology and Scripture, they grew into rigid doctrinal affirmations of required beliefs. Believers became known less by their deeds and lifestyle (like apostolic Christians) and more by whether they avowed the right things. Later, institutional Christianity focused on creeds that must be believed to be a church member in good standing. That is partly how doctrine replaced practice as what mattered most. While church councils shaped consensus, one thing is quite clear: creeds focused on doctrine, not practice.

CHRISTENDOM

It would not be reasonable to discuss history of the Christian religion without mentioning the Roman Catholic Church. Whether or not you agree with its claims of apostolic succession, its legacy pre-dates other segments of Christianity. My use of the term "Christendom" refers to its initial meaning around the 12th century, the Vatican's church-state phase, but obviously much has changed. However, Soren Kierkegaard (1813-1855) said, "Life can only be understood by looking backward, but it must be lived looking forward." In my view, carefully considering history remains vital to understanding where we are today.

BROAD SOCIAL CHANGE

For perspective, it is always difficult for those caught up in a sociological shift, like the change of Christianity from spiritual movement to official religion, to grasp what is happening while it is happening. The social dynamics of today's 21st century America similarly challenge anyone in their midst to accurately describe them, though many have tried.

While the Vatican claims about half of all Christian believers worldwide, one of the largest religious groups in modern America is the growing number of lapsed Catholics—those raised in that church but who no longer attend for various reasons. Adults leaving the church of their youth is a broader issue. The current ecclesiastical exodus also includes many Protestants who no longer attend the church where they grew up, or any at all. Why are so many people leaving churches despite religious appeals to attend? Maybe former churchgoers no longer see

46

the point of attending. Maybe it is a gradual recognition by some believers, and increasingly their offspring, that going to church no longer has any substantive connection to following Jesus.

At a time when membership in social or fraternal organizations has also taken a downturn, churches may increasingly be seen as just another group, using Jesus as a namesake, but little else. A common refrain among some of the disenchanted is that they like Jesus, but not his church. Thus, it may have become increasingly clear, to at least some former churchgoers, that what they personally experienced was largely a superficial religion that lacks the purpose-beyond-self of authentic spirituality (following Jesus). Without a spiritual connection, church is just another demand made upon busy modern families.

Despite the problems we see throughout the evolution of institutional Christendom, I believe it is still possible to follow Jesus in almost any ecclesiastical organization that claims Christ as the Messiah. True, some churches may make it much harder than others to progress from a new convert to a mature disciple who can show others how to live for Jesus. But, Paul's words to believers to persevere regardless of their circumstances still resonate today (1 Cor 7:20-24).

We are not called by God to be successful as the world defines achievements, but rather to be faithful—regardless of where we find ourselves, even if our church does not help us pursue spiritual goals.

Who among us can control all our life's situations or how we might love God and serve others? What we can impact is how we respond to life as a follower of Jesus, as someone who takes seriously what Christ commanded, taught, and practiced. While not all churchgoers may want to follow Christ, any churchgoer can still become a Christ-follower.

THE REFORMATION

When Martin Luther began what is now called the Reformation in 1517, he renounced the sale of indulgences, the predatory practice of selling get-out-of-purgatory guarantees to raise money.

Though he did not dispute Rome's stance on church-state issues, Luther did help bring the Bible to the language of the common people; other translations followed. It is, of course, easy to target the Roman Catholic Church for criticism, but as I overheard whispered at one church conference, "We Protestants are more Catholic than we like to admit." Let us examine some key legacies.

CLERGY-LAITY

While the New Testament discusses difference between members of the body of Christ (Rom 12:4-8, 1 Cor 12:14-30, and Eph 4:11-12), the Vatican's priesthood owes much to Judaism. The specialization of the Aaronic priesthood, those dedicated to serving God in the temple, is obvious when examining Scripture. For Catholic priests to be the sole conduit to God makes sense in that regard. But the apostle Peter makes a broader point by saying that believers are "a chosen people, a royal priesthood, a holy nation, a people belonging to God" (1 Peter 2:10). Thus, giftedness, not church designation, dictates the various ways in which we all can serve our heavenly father.

SYNCRETISM

Throughout church history, some observances or beliefs have been adapted from the broader culture and incorporated into the church for religious purposes. Such commingling of the secular with the sacred is called syncretism. Some of these practices help bring an ancient faith to a modern world. But it is important to recognize how various church traditions developed.

Some church observances or rituals have become such entrenched traditions that they have become almost sacred and thus unquestionable. Originally published in 2002, the 2008 edition of *Pagan Christianity?* by Frank Viola and George Barna, outlines the cultural origins of some current religious practices. Since many topics were sensitive, this religious publisher put a blunt disclaimer in the book's beginning to defend its content which might offend some readers.

Christmas was originally a pagan festival that was turned into a Christian celebration. Some find that the commercialization of the holiday detracts from its potentially spiritual significance.

The traditional concept of hell as "eternal, conscious torment" came from Greek philosophy. Plato thought that the threat of punishment after this life would help keep social order. Some find this simplistic carrot (heaven) and stick (hell) theology offensive. Others find that the traditional church concept of a loving God torturing unbelievers forever does not make sense given biblical language that describes those who perish (John 3:16).

It is difficult to accept or follow Jesus if you lose sight of him in a cultural fog or get side-tracked by church teachings that have little to do with putting into practice what was said by God's son. Like one author said, "It's not what I don't understand about the Bible that bothers me, it's what I do understand and don't want to do." Rejecting God makes most sense to those who have no desire to respect or willingly submit to a higher authority than themselves in today's narcissism.

SALVATION = CHURCH

Just as a person's nature (genetics) and nurture (how they were raised) shape their being, so did the institutional counterparts of the Roman Catholic Church shape its Protestant offspring. It would be inaccurate to say that the Vatican has not dealt with several theological issues that needed attention, but how those situations developed still matters. Understanding how things happened can help us move forward responsibly while avoiding some of the same problems.

Subtly important among many sectarian beliefs is the core concept that salvation depends on their church, not upon Christ. Paraphrasing that doctrine: "There is no salvation outside the church." Church membership became the major emphasis because there is no salvation outside their specific church. Like much Roman Catholic ecclesiology, some biblical basis for this exists. But in the case of Catholicism, the Pope, rather than Jesus, has become "mediator between God and man" (1 Tim 2:5). In contrast, while first becoming a believer remains the foundation of a relationship between any person and God, that spiritual relationship, not organizational membership in any church, is what will matter at Judgment.

It is not possible to overstate the importance of the concept that there is no salvation outside a particular church affiliation. This institutional preeminence provides the authority for churches to tell people what they must do to go to heaven. Fear of hell, especially in earlier times, likely drove some of the uneducated to church because of the prospect of a fiery eternity.

As churchgoers became more literate and able to think about things not mentioned in their church, but taught by Jesus, the gap between going to church and following Jesus became clearer to some. Once churchgoers realize that leaders may not have their best interests as their primary focus, it is easier to recognize religious rituals as being secondary, not primary, matters of faith. Still, who likes to think that their religion misconstrued what Jesus commanded and taught?

CONFESSION

The Catholic Church's seven sacraments (Baptism, Confirmation, the Eucharist, Penance, Anointing of the Sick, Matrimony, and Holy Orders) benefit the church more than parishioners because they keep individuals dependent upon their institution's gate-keeper priests. I focus on one specific sacrament that could contribute more to those who want to sincerely follow Jesus.

Penance, more often known as Confession, helps individual believers and their priests examine the gap between belief and practice. In recent years the practice of Confession has diminished. Catholic practice relies upon an individual seeking guidance rather than upon a spiritual sibling pointing out gaps between belief and practice that only an intimate relationship might identify.

The Protestant counterpart to the Catholic sacrament is informal. James 5:16 directs the practice of confessing our sins to one another—something lacking in many institutional churches. The Lord's Prayer and elsewhere (Luke 17:3-4) affirm the importance of personal confession and forgiveness. Without spiritual siblings on the same journey, committed to encouragement and timely admonition, it is easy to avoid discussing one's own developmental status. Who likes to discuss our shortcomings or even acknowledge them? Like the 12-step saying that "we are as sick as our secrets," believers who do not consider their own spiritual status can suffer from life-threatening wounds. To be clear, the gap between belief and practice does need to be examined to help gauge spiritual status.

But, standard directions for penance have limited personal impact compared to the intimacy of knowledgeable critiques from those spiritually closest to you. Chapter 7, "Loving Others," goes into greater detail. The early church depended upon small groups. Large gatherings had their purpose, but the foundations of their faith often came from spiritual intimacy with one another.

GEO-POLITICS

History leaves no doubt about the Vatican's impact on past political developments. The Crusades were wars fought in the name of Christ, as armies journeyed to the Holy Lands and back. Popes held significant secular power and impacted society through their connections with political leaders. When King Henry VIII split from the Vatican, he did not eliminate the overlap of church and state, but only replaced the Roman Catholic Church with the Church of England (Anglican).

While we might question the biblical basis for such theopolitical involvement, facts remain. History records religious persecutions and many bloody wars fought in the name of God by colonizing powers such as England, France, Spain, and Portugal. In contrast, the Gospels show that Jesus was not militant. Those who focus on warrior-Jesus in the book of Revelation and treat end-times apocalyptic symbolism as the dominant characterization of God's son, substantially downplay the plain language of Matthew, Mark, Luke, and John about the Prince of Peace.

European explorers from "Christian" nations did not treat indigenous people kindly. To say that such an approach glorified God would be a stretch by any theological imagination. Briefly, God's kingdom is not "of this world," but that concept has not kept various church leaders from trying to influence secular government for their own purposes, a practice that continues today.

Moving Forward

Constantine has few defenders these days, but the Vatican, of course, rigorously replies to its critics, including those supposedly in its ranks. For an internal critique of Rome by someone who continues his childhood legacy with an ongoing claim to be Catholic, read at least the introductory seven pages to the 2002 book titled, *Why I Am A Catholic*, by Garry Wills. Those who know this author's writings and scholarly credentials probably also know of his 2000 book, *Papal Sin, Structures of Deceit*. Wills pulls no punches as his nuanced criticism points out specific failures within Catholicism. However, Rome's approved literature often makes clear the ultimate sanction against Catholics for apostate (unsanctioned) views: excommunication. But the issues raised by Wills might provoke an informed discussion among lapsed Catholics who might wonder why they lost faith in the religion of their youth. One more recent issue is discussed early in the next chapter.

4.
Churchianity

Sometimes religious institutions hurt their devoted followers which is a conflict of interests.

Churchianity focuses on institutional goals, like building up its numbers without attention to each churchgoer's individual spiritual status. Just going to weekly religious services does not necessarily help each churchgoer become more like Jesus, though it can help. While churches offer many benefits to its members, unless they help new converts become more like Jesus, they fail in their most basic mission: making disciples, authentic followers of God's son.

The institutionalization of religion often results in a top-down organization; those in power try to protect themselves and their institution from accountability. Jesus condemned the same thing at length in Matthew 23. He criticized "teachers of the law and Pharisees," and repeatedly called them "hypocrites." Why? Verse 3 says, "they do not practice what they preach."

To cite a well-known and public example, the sexual molestation of children by some Roman

Catholic clergy caused many Catholics to question their churches' priorities and others to discredit God. How could such a thing happen? Religious leaders forgot their followers—spiritual shepherds forgot their sheep! Church authorities tried to protect their institutional brand instead of the vulnerable youth in their care, thus betraying both them and their trusting family.

To be fair, other organizations have also been exposed as having similar problems with sexual abuse among its trusted leaders. But given the Vatican's hierarchy and oversight role, its failure to stop known pedophiles from victimizing other children makes Rome's negligence even worse.

CONFLICT OF INTERESTS

The widespread religious coverups of criminal behavior discussed above illustrates only one way that institutional goals have trumped individual interests. Other basic conflicts emerge between churches who want to build membership numbers while many believers have an eternal goal in mind.

At the end of this earthly life, each believer expects to be found faithful, but Jesus has specific guidance about those who will be welcomed into his eternal kingdom. Judgment Day will focus on each person, not on churches. Matthew 7:21-29 and 25:31-46 explain that those who claim "Jesus as Lord" will be evaluated individually. Carefully consider the following verses. We will "all stand before God's judgment seat" (Rom 14:10). Rather than judge others, "wait until the Lord comes. He will bring to light what is hidden in darkness and will expose the motive of men's hearts" (1 Cor 4:5). We "must all appear before the judgment seat of Christ" (2 Cor 5:10).

The basic organization of the pulpit/pew church service is designed to be efficient from an institutional standpoint. But how can such a group setting be effective for meeting the spiritual needs of various individuals who might be struggling and need help, but be reluctant or afraid to ask? One message can reach large numbers of churchgoers. Mass media multiplies that ratio, but often focuses upon making converts rather than helping new Christians become mature disciples. Growth requires spiritual apprenticeships because each babe in Christ faces their own challenges.

God's assessment of each of us at the end of time will be based upon our individual situations, not on our institutional affiliation. Our thoughts, words, and actions, when taken together, define a believer's relationships with God and others. Churches often claim to be God's representatives on earth, but their institutional roles sometimes work at cross purposes to this book's premise: churches should help individual believers follow Jesus as their Lord and Master. When leaders do what best serves their institutional efficiency, rather than what most effectively helps their members, what God instituted as the church has become something less than he intended.

My Definition of Churchianity

The term "churchianity" has been around since the late 19th century when periodicals used the term to describe—in unflattering terms—what some thought had become of Christianity. Thus, my use of this pejorative is not original. But I am redefining this term to call out the decline of a spiritual movement originally dedicated to following Jesus. Various parts of Christianity center around their calls to come to church, thus churchianity, rather than calls to follow Jesus.

There is a big difference between those early spiritual communities of Christ-followers and today's institutions with what amounts to local franchises of churchgoers. Periodic assemblies in a sacred space to affirm core beliefs may feel good to those churchgoers, but that is not enough. The actual practice, if any, of what Jesus commanded, taught, and exemplified must take place outside a church building's walls. It matters how believers behave in the broader community. Such behavior with others must be built upon a serious spiritual relationship with their God.

The parable of the Good Samaritan describes a secular setting where religious leaders pass by an injured man (Luke 10:25-37). Nobody got involved—except for one man, who was not identified as a religious leader. Any faith community whose religion consists mainly of attendance at proper events in proper settings has lost its way. Those who serve Christ's heavenly father must do so where they live, not just where they assemble in sacred space. Keeping the entire practice of faith in a church building is like placing a lamp under a basket where it illuminates nothing (Matt 5:15-16). Jesus taught about faith in a way that totally encompasses a believer's life, their decision-making, and their being. Though often imperfect, early believers tried to follow Jesus.

Another aspect of churchianity involves resource allocation: what church leaders prioritize in their budgets. In considering personal charities, I evaluate the percentage spent on administration compared to that spent on their advertised purpose. Some highly publicized appeals for those in obvious need end up funneling a large percentage of their take into overhead. More to the point, at one church conference an African explained to me in private how one in-country meeting to discuss helping their poor was held in a high-end resort—a clear disconnect.

Annual budgets reveal priorities. The allocation of religious resources to the maintenance and operation of the physical building where churchgoers assemble is not necessarily bad. Like a home mortgage and related costs are often a large part of a family's budget, many churches devote substantial funds to their facilities. If their building has been around for some time and has been paid off, much of their congregational assets consist of their real estate value.

Besides a meeting place, salary and benefits make up most of the rest of many church budgets. Effort devoted to sermon preparation, delivery, and associated tasks for each week's Sunday morning services, consumes much of any pulpit minister's time. In business settings with cost allocation plans that apportion staff time to each cost-center's purpose, such a connection would be obvious. Many churches spend most of their money on their buildings and staff, not on others.

Having a dedicated building and staff can be seen as self-serving if their main purpose is to theologically entertain regular churchgoers rather than necessarily helping struggling believers. How can those who claim to follow Jesus show the world what they believe if most of their institutional resources focus on self-serving superficialities? That does not mean that a church should not own property, but for new churches just starting out, the main question should not be buying a building, but what will best help those believers who hunger and thirst for righteousness to follow Jesus?

CONTRASTING CHRISTIANITY WITH CHURCHIANITY

The book of Acts refers to followers of Christ as "the Way" (Acts 9:2, 19:9, 19:23). The term Christianity for the new religion came much later. The root word for Christian comes from a Greek expression meaning Christ-person or Christ-follower, and appears only three times in the New Testament (Acts 11:26, 26:28, and 1 Pet. 4:16). Christ-person implies a relationship, a member of a spiritual family based upon a vertical relationship with God and a horizontal relationship with other believers. Today, the word Christian has lost some of its original meaning.

Even social critic Bill Maher, in his 2008 documentary *Religulous*, distinguished between being Christian and being Christlike. Maher makes fun of many aspects of institutional Christianity, but also includes a revealing comment. After interviewing one small group of believers, he thanked them for their cooperation and for being Christlike, not just Christian. That suggests a big difference in meaning between those two words—not all Christians act like Christ.

This book uses the term "churchianity" to refer to an institutionalized form of the original faith. Churchianity focuses on its own organizational religion regardless of its use of any sacred terms in its name. The term "Christianity" refers to the relationship-based faith in Christ as God's son.

Breakaway groups may start out seeking to come closer to Christianity, but almost invariably wind up as another version of churchianity. The Protestant Reformation illustrates this concept. Starting out to make needed improvements, it eventually lapsed back into some of the behavioral patterns it had earlier rejected. When Christianity loses sight of Jesus, it degenerates into churchianity.

Obviously, no Christian congregation or sect ever decides to advocate churchianity. No church leader would ever say, "let's change the basic core of our faith from a relationship with God into an institutional bureaucracy." The shift is subtle and gradual. Further, just because a particular denomination largely embodies churchianity does not keep groups or individuals within it from continuing to practice the faith as originally intended (Christianity). However, being surrounded by a culture of churchianity can make it easy for an individual believer or a group of believers to be drawn into it. After all, there are some benefits: structure brings security, belonging to an institution is attractive, and organizations, even the most bureaucratic ones, can sometimes accomplish things that a more informal collection of individuals cannot. But the loss of deeper relationships hampers personal growth. Also, legalism, bureaucracy, and institutionalism are condemned by the prophets, by the New Testament writers, and by Jesus. When an institution becomes more important than its individual members, both can easily lose their way.

Jesus values even one lost sheep (Matt 18:12–14). Instead, churchianity values its sectarian doctrines, its practices, and its own organizational identity in the face of any criticism about how it treats members. Any shepherd who fails to help his sheep learn to closely follow the Good Shepherd enables them to wander away where Satan prowls, ready to devour them (1 Pet 5:8).

This tendency toward churchianity is why it is crucial for every church leader and indeed every believer to periodically examine their spiritual attitudes, perspectives, and practices to affirm the importance of a healthy, Christ-centered community. But organizations depend on their leaders, who tend to perpetuate the status quo. Power often corrupts. Few powerful people ever willingly give up their positional authority to overtly reject their organizational emphasis on churchianity.

In any faith journey, there will be times when converts stumble or stagnate in their spiritual development. New believers should be alerted that this might happen. At some point all believers will encounter difficulties and might even stray (1 Cor 10:13). These cautions should lead to serious discussions, even among the most spiritual (Rom 7:15-25). All believers are called to be part of a spiritual community of like-minded people striving to encourage each other, to hold each other accountable, and to become more like Jesus. When we lose sight of such purposes, Christianity becomes churchianity. Church leaders will almost never admit that they have neglected their flock, so individual churchgoers need to be vigilant as they continue their own spiritual journey. Are their leaders helping them or not? That is a very personal question.

When organizations that have morphed into churchianity are criticized, they tend to cling to their own institutional model as if it were sacred. These churches provide their members a sense of security because they offer a guaranteed entry to heaven and avoidance of hell. Such churchgoers have been persuaded that they are right and righteous. After all, who continues to hold on to beliefs unless they are convinced that they are correct? In response, please consider an old saying that "it ain't what you don't know that gets you into trouble. It's what you know for sure that just ain't so."

MERE CHURCHGOERS

Churchianity produces mere churchgoers while Christianity yields Christ-followers. While many of us cannot see problems with our own spiritual lives, we somehow often focus on where others might be misguided. That may be why Jesus discussed the "beam versus splinter" problem (Matt 7:3-5, KJV). One physical brother of Jesus echoes that sentiment when discussing the purpose of looking into the mirror of Scripture. James cautions against going away and forgetting what we saw in ourselves, thus forgetting to act upon God's message (Jas 1:23-24).

The following theoretical comparisons will not apply everywhere but illustrate how I view the differences between churchianity and Christianity. All analytical modeling only serves as word pictures designed to help readers see what they might otherwise be missing. These suggestions should not be used as a checklist for any believer's own spiritual health, but rather are intended to prompt serious discussion about their applicability. What do you think about such characterizations? Do they make sense? Do they apply to some others, but not you?

Mere churchgoers are more likely to:

- Experience superficial socialization which is enjoyable, and beneficial, but not the same as the "one-another" spiritual connection outlined in Scripture (see chapter 7). To get to really know someone and their complete situation, it takes time, effort, and interactions beyond the casual chats that happen in most church settings. To help another believer with a problem almost always requires first understanding them, before they need help.

- Focus their religious practices on building-oriented rather than home-based faith. Their leaders value regular attendance, being there whenever church building doors are open. Check-list adherence will not lead to a life "in Christ" if a believer does not live their faith elsewhere. Living for Jesus involves more than periodic rituals.

- Emphasize orthodoxy/right belief without a corresponding emphasis on orthopraxy/right practice. Despite their good intentions, what many Christian churches have in common remains a lack of emphasis on having their members follow Jesus each day.

- Stress church membership in response to the Great Commission rather than modeling Jesus in response to the two Greatest Commandments (see chapter 9). When evangelical churches minimize efforts to foster spiritual growth after conversion, they limit the development needed by each convert to continue their path toward maturity.

- Know God only in the context of a church setting and thus are not able to take their faith home to apply it to everyday life in their family and at work. Sometimes such people put on a happy face when going to church despite whatever real struggles they may be facing.

- Seem unable to gauge the difference between their church doctrines or statements of faith and what Jesus explicitly said would really matter at judgment (see Matthew 7 and 25).

- Have leaders who focus on attendance and finances rather than on the spiritual depth of their flock. Rather than being shepherds looking after each sheep, they tend to be business managers more interested in what they can count, not what spiritually counts.

- Have leaders who believe that bigger is better rather than working toward creating an extended family-like spiritual community that genuinely looks after each other and takes shared responsibility for each other's maturation. Sadly, if churchgoers become isolated, they are much more easily deceived by Satan's tactics to separate them from their faith.

- Have leaders who place members in church roles that serve institutional needs rather than recognizing and developing each member's knowledge, skills, and abilities to further their individual growth. Such mismatched members can more easily become burned out by their "volunteer" church work while their own maturation process stagnates.

These subjective comparisons cover a broad spectrum of any organization's characteristics. But they may help individuals decide if they are being distracted, or deceived by Satan. His tactics use culture and bureaucracy against God's people to keep them from following Jesus. Like fishermen who use different kinds of bait to catch different kinds of fish, Satan uses varied approaches in demonic attempts to sidetrack different types of believers from spiritual growth.

Please do not think that there is a list of rules to follow to be a genuine Christian organization. That would be falling into the same trap as I am critiquing! It is up to believers to follow Jesus, keeping in mind that God is the one who makes the final judgment while we are called to do our best with sincere humility and grace. Remember, churches may not help, so every believer should periodically assess their own spiritual life.

Churches tend to measure everything that can be counted, yet often fail to recognize the most important aspects of the Christianity which cannot be counted. The priority remains development of each individual believer's spirituality, something qualitative, not easily evaluated.

Have you ever been around a new convert "on fire for the Lord" who gradually becomes just another churchgoer? After having had their enthusiasm squelched, for example, such a person descends from Christianity into churchianity. How does that normally happen? How did the person who converted from unbelief to follow Jesus become content to just go to church? Experiences vary, but mine was often that an institutional focus on conversion, on gaining new church members, was not followed by an emphasis on individual growth. Spiritual seedlings sometimes die, which is not unexpected, given the parable of the soils (Matt 13:3-9, 18-23). But should their spiritual community have ignored challenges facing vulnerable babes in Christ? It makes no sense to keep welcoming people in the front door if they are allowed to gradually slip out the back.

WHY CHURCHIANITY CONTINUES

First, some perpetually immature churchgoers never progress toward maturity because they have not learned or been taught how to spiritually feed themselves. Churchianity results from such an unhealthy dependence if those in the pews depend only on the pulpit to feed them. In such cases, those who sit in the pews come to church to be fed by a cleric who dispenses theological narrative, leads group rituals, and orchestrates liturgical routines. To be sure, those who make their living from the pulpit have little choice. Presenting good sermons is difficult and takes preparation. But any genuine spiritual apprenticeship, like Jesus offered to those who followed him, would take much more time than is available for individual ministry. Nurturing such development requires involvement in each believer's life—sheep need a shepherd who looks after each one.

Second, while some religious leaders admit that their policies and procedures might need review, many do not want to admit the need for serious reflection. Some proclaim certainty, as if they had divine insights that others do not. Their sincerity plays a key role in convincing others to follow their views of what God wants. In any case, the process of helping churchgoers become Christ-followers is often quite messy which some leaders find unacceptable or unworkable.

Third, churchgoers sometimes just enjoy social gatherings, which have many benefits. Personal interests benefit from social networking; word-of-mouth connections may provide commercial opportunities. But, members working the crowd for personal gain is not the same as keeping up with other people's lives to be able to offer help when needed. Timing is critical when spiritual siblings need help. It takes being aware of another believer's personal situation to know when and how to appropriately offer help. Regardless of such good intentions, some people see today's churchgoers as socially or politically networked, not spiritually engaged in following Jesus.

Fourth, for many in older generations, a sense of cultivated guilt makes church-going a necessity. These people need to attend church to feel comfortable going about the rest of their lives. This may not have anything to do with living for Jesus or submitting themselves to their Lord and Master. Church-going for such people can be mainly cosmetic. Since sermons do not always fit their situation, they do not always benefit from pulpit messages, apart from checking a box that makes them feel better because they have done their religious duty by going to church.

Fifth, many adults were indoctrinated into their parents' religion as children. Visceral connections from early childhood often continue throughout life. Some lapsed Catholics, for example, cannot escape the lessons imprinted in their impressionable young minds about the need to participate in various sacraments. Childhood fears about hell often remain to some degree. If you married into a church-going family, it is sometimes easier to become a member than to rock the proverbial boat. Following along with your spouse's religion will often help keep the peace at home.

Sixth, it is a common occurrence that, as we grow older, our brains and hearts both become resistant to new ideas. Change can become difficult. Much like our cardiovascular system can become compromised through the hardening of its arteries, many lose religious flexibility. In the same way, churchianity becomes entrenched as the way of thinking about what it means to be a Christian. Once someone has bought into and lived that idea, it is difficult to change their theological mind. They have become invested in it. It is what they have known. It becomes their religious identity that they will guard with their entire being. Churchgoers often think that any criticism of their beliefs is an attack on God or on their church's guarantee of heaven. So, they will always defend it even when they do not fully understand what they believe or why.

Finally, it is difficult for many churchgoers to think about their religious beliefs without viewing it from their sectarian perspective. Satan's divide and conquer tactic has worked quite well to keep all believers from coming together to serve God. What would happen if all those who claim Jesus as Lord and Master came together and put away relatively minor doctrinal differences to focus on loving God and loving others? What could be accomplished to glorify our Creator?

PROBLEMS SOMETIMES HAVE SOLUTIONS

While I cannot fully summarize centuries of religious misconduct in this discussion, I can point out potential problems and suggest a framework for analysis. Not every church is the same, so each reader should carefully consider the problems and solutions suggested here. One way to assess your own situation is by deciding whether your spiritual growth is helped or hindered by your own organizational setting. While it is possible to grow in any situation, some organizations make it more difficult than others. Ask yourself: is your church helping its members to become more Christlike or hindering them? Does anyone know if such efforts are successful? How can spiritual status be determined if it is never discussed? If there is no theological intimacy, how can any believer confess sin to one another, encourage one another, bear each other's burdens, or seek advice from one another? Is your own maturation due to or despite your religious setting? That is an uncomfortable—but useful—self-assessment. Nobody else can do it; it is up to you. Like most institutions, many individuals find it difficult to change and so often remain the same.

Each believer's status and growth should concern the entire church body. Twelve-step programs target a particular problem for an often-self-selected small group; the classic use of this approach involves addiction to alcohol. Such groups focus on a problem common to every member, encourage acknowledgment of individual issues, and help each other on their own road to recovery. Christ-followers have a similar journey that also lasts a lifetime. Given the unique nature of temptations, each church should help its believers with their self-assessment and own journey toward becoming more Christlike. Discipleship involves personal sacrifice, submission to God, and commitment. It is a process, not an event; it is a distance race, not a sprint.

AN EXCEPTION TO EVERY RULE

Not all churches succumb to an exclusively institutional focus. Not all churches become an end in themselves. Not all churches are run by business managers rather than spiritually inclined servant-leaders. But if you are unable to tell whether you have spiritual siblings, you probably do not, especially if you are only accustomed to superficial conversations rather than the type of exchange intended by the New Testament's "one-another" verses (see Chapter 7, "Loving Others"). While casual conversations have their purpose in religious settings, they do not replace intimacy. Ironically, at a time when sexual intimacy seems pervasive, sociologists say that people are lonelier than ever. Social media does not effectively replace human interaction and existential angst appears rampant if increasing suicides are any indication. Churches should provide a safe way for members to develop the spiritual intimacy needed for ongoing reflection and repentance.

The ultimate organizational irony is this: if religious institutions took better care of their individual churchgoers, they very likely would achieve their goals for growth. The whole is much more than the sum of its parts, because a healthy group of members makes for a healthy church. When any part of the church body suffers, it needs help, because a healthy body can best focus on any part that needs healing. That requires intimate connections. Without periodic check-ups, how does anyone know if they are truly healthy? Do people just hope to stay healthy, or do they check with someone whose judgment can be relied upon to give a trustworthy assessment when they have problems? Spiritual wounds cry out for immediate, appropriate attention. Many traumatic events leave invisible injuries that require long-term care for proper healing.

MOVING FORWARD

Christ has not gotten lost in every religious group claiming his name, but it is certainly a characteristic of many such groups. Churches that emphasize a sectarian focus often have largely eliminated following Jesus Christ from their orthopraxy, how they practice their faith. In such cases, building on a foundation of sand will not end well for those churchgoers (Matt 7:26-29).

Conversion from unbelief should begin a lifestyle commitment to God. Should responsiveness to our Creator be limited only to periodic gatherings in sacred spaces, or should it be a 24/7 journey? Religious organizations tend to become an end in themselves if they do not intentionally monitor and critique themselves. It is no surprise that many faith tribes emphasize showing up in their church pews rather than living for Christ, becoming more like Jesus.

What if all Christian leaders began to echo Christ? What if their common message was to follow Jesus? Too often religious leaders today look for creative ways to increase attendance. Instead, religious leaders who claim to represent Christ should want their churchgoers to become more like Jesus and thus glorify God. Humble, sacrificial, purpose-beyond-self living best honors our Creator and illustrates our heavenly father's purpose for all his adopted children. Without that spiritual goal as a religious organization's top priority, it becomes much more likely that Christianity will continue to devolve into churchianity, which takes many ecumenical shapes. As a result, rather than treating Jesus as Lord and Master, some churchgoers may just want him to be their Savior. They may just want a ticket to heaven and to avoid hell, but from how I understand Scripture, they will be disappointed.

5.
Christianity

Authentic Christianity has some verifiable characteristics; carefully look for them.

Gradually stepping away from an evangelical congregation that I faithfully served for over thirty years helped me develop insights that I might not have otherwise recognized as a church leader. My self-imposed exile helped me recognize the symptoms of an institutional framework destined to fail many believers. It dawned on me that instead of being among those Christ-followers joining Jesus in eternity, on Judgment Day some churchgoers might hear, "I never knew you." Why? Such individuals did not take Jesus at his word and their religious institutions did not help.

Earlier, I did not know what to do and was part of the problem. Now I understand. Conversion is not enough; discipleship is what matters to God. Churchgoing is not enough; following Jesus is what matters. Institutional religion can unknowingly stand in the way of spirituality. Our Creator desires relationships with and among his children. Christianity without such godly connections between believers is like a superficial church social. Christ's church, his body, exists to help each of its human parts become more like Jesus during the difficult challenges of this life.

ANALYTICAL APPROACH

During my administrative career in Alaskan state government, I learned two analytical concepts that can be used to evaluate churches: performance audits and budget priorities. No church gets it all right and no church gets it all wrong, but the problem with many religious institutions is their failure to grasp a core responsibility: helping individual churchgoers become Christ-followers.

Performance audits of any program begin by reviewing its legal purpose to evaluate it. To consider Christianity, I summarize what Scripture says to determine what God intends. The Hebrew Bible's two Greatest Commandments, both affirmed and applied by Jesus, explain what matters most. Many scriptures relate to each believer's vertical relationship with God and horizontal relationships with others. Thus, each of the two Greatest Commandments deserves its own detailed explanation (see Chapter 6, "Loving God," and Chapter 7, "Loving Others").

Priorities have an impact on what any organization achieves. Some examples offer insights. After a mass casualty event, triage dictates that the injured need to be divided into groups: those who need immediate attention (to keep them alive), those who will die (regardless of what is done next), and those who can wait (with minor injuries). Medical professionals understand the need for such priorities that help save as many as possible when facing resource constraints. Some churches or believers do not recognize priorities; they do not know how to face life's challenges. But, the wise virgins took oil for their lamps to prepare for the unexpected (Matt 25:1-13).

From an institutional standpoint, there is never enough time or money to do everything. What gets done and what gets left undone leaves a visible legacy for those claiming to serve Jesus. Since the garden of Eden, Satan has tried to distract children of God from following instructions by questioning God's clearest messages. In one sense, that is a matter of deciding upon priorities. Should follow-ing Jesus be the priority? I say yes. Remember how Adam and Eve ignored one simple instruction to avoid "the tree of the knowledge of good and evil" (Gen 2:17)? Their disobedience continues when people decide to pursue their own choices, not what God has explicitly said.

While many things may seem important, if the highest priority is not following Jesus, as his early disciples did, then other issues inevitably take cen-ter stage. Even the best of intentions can sound good, but end up being bad. Evangelical leaders who prioritize making new converts, but do not help those "babes in Christ" grow spiritually have neglected teaching them to obey everything that Jesus commanded (Matt 28:20). Without help, how can new churchgoers mature toward loving God and others? Moving from unbelief to belief remains important, but what if they become like those in Laodicea, "neither hot nor cold" (Rev 3:15), because they have not grown? Chapter 9, "The Great Omission," discusses the need for helping converts become disciples.

Religious leaders who try to shape secular policy in the name of God comprise another major distraction from God's priorities. This present world has a shelf-life and will come to an end. What matters is each believer's responsiveness to God, not whether any government resembles a religious community's values. Remember, worldly values differ from those that will go beyond this world (1 Cor 5:9-13). Chapter 10, "The Seduction of Partisan Politics," goes into detail.

How Christianity Lost Some Meaning

The terms Christian and Christianity have lost some of their original meanings. Their denotation, or dictionary definition, remains. But their connotation, or cultural meaning, has been diluted by an increased association with televangelist fund-raisers, theopolitical activists, blatant hypocrisy, cults, and more. Religion used to be widespread; many books now refer to a post-Christian era. Some say that Satan's greatest trick was to convince many that he does not exist, but besides that, his next best tactic has been to make a mockery of God and his people in as many ways as possible.

To help churchgoers become Christ-followers, it is important to separate direct commands (like the two Greatest Commandments) from sectarian or derived doctrines (like "original" versus actual sin, or everything that happens is part of "God's plan"). Further, before concentrating upon the epistles, the Gospels should be mastered. While some label the Apostle Paul as *the* Christian theologian, Jesus has all authority. To fully understand what the apostles say in their letters, believers need to first understand Christ's foundational, multi-layered teachings laid out in the Gospels. Without such an understanding, some believers might confuse apostolic letters as pre-eminent rather than than extensions of what Jesus taught.

AUTHENTIC CHRIST-FOLLOWERS

My attempt to offer spiritual insights about authentic Christianity consists not of doctrinal absolutes, but of practical guidelines. Jesus often spoke in open-ended parables, with layers of meaning about how to respond. Thus, the following suggestions might give believers some ideas about how to discuss their spiritual status with others on the same journey. Textbook learning will always come up short when compared to the sharing of actual situations among believers.

Just as math story problems, law school hypotheticals, or management case studies all have some instructive value, what follows may be a useful starting point for small group discussions among spiritual siblings. Naturally, those willing to help other believers become more like Jesus do not all have the same perspective. But those who view their own spiritual maturity as a long-term goal worth working toward, should be willing to discuss the following provocative suggestions.

Authentic Christ-followers are more likely to:

- Nurture spiritual fruit (Gal 5:22-23) throughout each day, rather than focus upon worship services. With this list (love, joy, peace, patience, kindness, goodness, faithfulness, gentleness, and self-control), the Apostle Paul echoes Jesus.

- Recognize and avoid chronic temptations. The ungodly attributes listed in Galatians 5:19-21 (and elsewhere) are warning signs that they will "not inherit the kingdom" if they engage in sexual immorality, idolatry, hatred, jealousy, rage, selfish ambition, envy, drunkenness, orgies, and the like. Each believer has their own vulnerability.

- Do their best to become part of an intimate spiritual community like the original concept of a church body with its many parts (Rom 12:3-8). Such an approach requires sustained effort outside of large gatherings. The various "one-another" verses in chapter 7 go into greater detail about what can be developed by those who commit themselves to a spiritual community. Even among only two or three, Jesus is there (Matt 18:20).

- Cultivate a personal passion for following Jesus, wholeheartedly, not just during church gatherings. That often means having a godly spouse or accountability partner where both help shape their lives toward God. They can better serve their heavenly father as they watch each other's spiritual back and help each other grapple with temptations.

- Recognize the reality-based nature of a life devoted to God, versus a superficial or image-based religiosity that masquerades as Christianity. Rather than just wearing their Sunday-best clothes for church, each day they try to put on Christ by how they live.

- Feel a personal accountability to Jesus rather than just a group responsibility to church. Such believers realize that any organization might let them down, so they take an intimate interest in their connection to Jesus with all that entails, rather than settling for whatever their organization prescribes. Such a dynamic must always be personal.

- Believe in a love-based grace that focuses on gratitude toward God rather than fear. Guilt can lead to avoidance of certain types of sin, but does not lead to *agape* love, the foundation for long-term responsiveness to God and thus to all service for others.

- Seek out someone more mature who can help them grow, rather than remaining content with church membership after their conversion from unbelief to belief. Just as each new "babe in Christ" looks for help from those more mature, they also hope to grow to the point where they can help those less mature, with the godly guidance they once sought.

- Willingly submit to Jesus as Lord and Master not just in public, but in quiet moments when nobody else will know their thoughts.

- Maintain the humility that comes from not thinking of themselves more highly than they ought, but rather thinking of themselves with sober judgment (Rom 12:3).

SPIRITUAL COMMUNITY?

New Testament narrative indicates the need for disciples to be in community, but if that gathering is focused on churchianity, not Christianity, problems easily develop. As John Wesley said, "the world needs more disciples, not more converts." Becoming a disciple is a matter of authentically following Jesus, doing what he said (Matt 7:21-29), not just joining a church.

Many evangelical churches tend to be heavy on their salvation protocol, but light on following Jesus. Some border on legalism, a religious *quid pro quo* (do this to be guaranteed heaven). They may not realize that they are advocating a variation on Pascal's Wager (i.e. if hell exists, we would be fools not to join a church to avoid it [my paraphrase], as if that would trick God).

Separate from any debates about controversial issues, most believers still agree that they fall short in authentically following what Jesus taught; we all miss the mark. One way to become more mature is to get help from spiritual siblings, believers on the same journey toward becoming more like Jesus. That takes a community focus, but if that community does not help its members, it is falling far short of what Christ intended. If a congregation is religious, and not spiritual, then it works against churchgoers learning to better follow Jesus as Lord and Master.

MOVING FORWARD

While applying the two Greatest Commandments to everyday life in Christ remains *the* priority, circumstances will vary for each believer. Responding to God will always be a personal matter. Chapters

6 and 7 ("Loving God" and "Loving Others") go into detail about the vertical and the horizontal aspects of a living faith.

The purpose of the two Greatest Commandments is to gradually shape each believer into becoming more like Jesus, the theme of chapter 8. Those who "hunger and thirst for righteousness" will be filled (Matt 5:6). Therefore, New Testament scriptures, especially the Gospels, provides ample multi-layered lessons about what to do and what to avoid.

Two distinct and deceptive diversions from following Jesus deserve their own chapters: Chapter 9, "The Great Omission," and Chapter 10, "The Seduction of Partisan Politics."

6.
Loving God

*The first Greatest Commandment is the foun-
dation of each believer's Christlike faith.*

This chapter will get more specific about certain
aspects of following Jesus (instead of just going to
church). Keep in mind that our God is spirit (John
4:24). Thus, balancing institutional religion with
the personal spirituality desired by our Creator (as
expressed in the first Greatest Commandment)
challenges all Christ-followers. To explain ways to
express love to God, this chapter approaches those
concepts by outlining the various spiritual disciplines often practiced throughout church history.
Still, each person who decides to become a child of
God, a follower of Jesus, must decide the extent,
depth, and particulars of their own faith journey.
Such introspection cannot be reduced to a formula,
but guidelines can help.

WHAT DOES IT MEAN TO LOVE GOD?

When Jesus affirms the first Greatest Commandment, "Love the Lord your God with all your heart

and with all your soul and with all your mind" (Matt 22:37), what does he mean? In our modern way of thinking, "heart" is usually emotion and "soul" usually refers to the spirit that survives after death—the essence of a person. But those words did not have those meanings in ancient Jewish thought. Instead, "heart" referred to a person's will; "soul" was the part of a human that is in God's image. "Mind" was the intellect. In other words, the phrase "heart, soul, and mind" make up the totality of a human being. In today's vernacular, Jesus might have said, "love God with everything you are" or "love God with every fiber of your being."

Adding the word "strength" to that phrase (see Mark 12:30 & Luke 10:27) emphasizes the idea that it takes work, and that you should pursue loving God with everything you have. It requires your best efforts. The Hebrew Bible contains several passages about the children of Israel offering their "first fruits," the best of their agricultural harvest, in thanksgiving to God—a clear priority. How can Christians do anything less than devote themselves fully to their Creator?

Thus, followers of Jesus are to love God with your whole selves, in all your thoughts and actions throughout your life. How can that happen? From early in the Christian tradition, this approach was often connected with practicing various spiritual disciplines—a series of attitudes and acts that were intended to help each believer love God with all their heart, soul, mind, and strength. Since God is spirit, it follows that our connection to the divine involves our spiritual life.

WHAT ARE SPIRITUAL DISCIPLINES?

Along with Jews before him, Jesus practiced what we call spiritual disciplines, but for different purposes. His unique status as both human (son of Man) and divine (son of God) changed their purpose from what they were to him to what they are for Christ-followers today. He had, for example, what Scripture calls "the Spirit without limit" (John 3:34), while his disciples needed to maintain their connection to the Holy Spirit, which can be quenched (1 Thess 5:19, KJV). Baptized to fulfill all righteousness (Matt 3:13-15), Jesus allowed himself to be treated like his later followers would be in their baptisms (Acts 2:38). He also practiced other disciplines, like prayer, but from a different perspective which still leaves us examples to follow.

To grow spiritually, Christ-followers must study and meditate on Scripture, as well as engage in prayer, fasting, worship, service, fellowship, and confession. For some believers, the quest for deeper connection to their Creator might include pursuing a simple life, practicing silence for periods of time, pilgrimages, or even monastic devotion. Any similar practice that helps us grow in our faith, strengthen our daily walk, and focus on loving God (the foundation for loving others), can be a very beneficial spiritual discipline. Many books have been written about each practice, so this brief overview will only be an appetizer inviting more extensive study.

However, it is important to emphasize that these spiritual disciplines do not ensure salvation or result in a special righteousness. They do not earn any unique favor with God, nor necessarily make their practitioners better than anyone else. They are intended as tools to help focus our minds on loving God more each day. Perhaps it is best to say that such spiritual disciplines are a response to God's love or blessings, a way to help us honor him in our daily lives. In that sense, such religious practices can help develop our core spiritual relationship. Why? Because they help cultivate responsiveness to our Creator, the ultimate goal of following Jesus. Also, if believers lose sight of God's grace, then legalism can creep into one's relationship with God.

These disciplines can be practiced alone or in groups, and doing both is important. Spiritual growth can be stunted if one's faith is practiced only in private or is practiced only in groups. Some disciplines lend themselves more to one setting than another. Worship is well-suited to corporate practice, while fellowship cannot take place in private. Confession can be practiced alone, directly to God, but it can be more cathartic when confiding to a spiritual sibling serving as an accountability partner (explored in Chapter 7, "Loving Others").

MEDITATING ON SCRIPTURE

Reading the Bible can have two main purposes: study and meditation. The first purpose is to learn about God, his ways, and what he expects of us as the best way to carry out our created purpose. Chapters 1 and 2 discussed studying Scripture, with ideas about how to go about it, as well as how to avoid some pitfalls of interpretation, both of which remain lifelong challenges.

The second purpose in reading the Bible is to use it as a form of meditation. Instead of merely studying the words, and using resources to look up history, language, and cultural issues, meditating on the word of God is a way to let your mind bask in the meaning of Scripture. Of course, prior personal study of any segment will give such a practice much more depth.

Many passages speak about the importance of meditating on or contemplating Scripture (e.g., Deut 11:18-21; Josh 1:8; Ps 1:2, 119:15-16; Phil 4:8; 1 Tim 4:13-15; and 2 Tim 2:7).

The purpose of meditating on God's word is to allow us to soak it in, to immerse ourselves in it, without doing too much intellectualizing or analyzing. It is a way to internalize Scripture in a different way than study. Meditation complements study.

How might we meditate on Scripture? There are several ways to do this, but all begin with choosing a passage. Even here, there are options. You could select a different translation than the one you normally use, or use different translations for different meditation sessions. You can work your way through a specific book in the Bible, or a chapter of a book, picking a passage, or even just a verse. You could even randomly pick one for each session. Many publications offer daily suggestions for such a practice.

Once you have your passage chosen, read the selection. Circle, underline, or highlight certain words that stand out, or perhaps diagram the passage using parts of speech if you learned how to do that in English grammar class.

In one sense, memorizing a passage is one of the oldest ways of helping you meditate on Scripture. Once memorized, you can recite the passage out loud or silently anytime you want. In that way, memorizing verses makes their message a part of you because you can immediately bring it to mind and apply its content to your life. By being able to recall such passages at will, you are also able to consider in more depth their layered meanings.

Out of a key passage, you could select one or two words to focus upon. You might ask yourself about their meanings, and then think at length about those particular words.

If you have artistic abilities, you might draw a specific word's meaning in graphic form, perhaps even something abstract or symbolic. Of course, certain passages lend themselves to prayer, so you could think through how you might use them as a prayer to meditate on their words. You could take each word in the passage, one at a time, and think about its meaning, and possible differences. Rewording the verse or passage might help you think about how its meaning might be different, changed, or clearer, considering its original language and cultural context.

Another method of meditation is to choose a passage with some sort of imagery, and then let your mind play that imagery out. Perhaps you choose the beginning of Psalm 23 "the Lord is my shepherd." What does it mean for God to be your shepherd? Why are you like a sheep, or are you? How is God like a shepherd? What does that word picture mean for those trying their best, with God's help, to be a follower of Jesus?

PRAYER

While many think of prayer as simply talking to God, a more complete definition goes further. Perhaps most people think that prayer is asking God for something (petitions or intercessions), but prayer in the Bible is far deeper and richer than that. Prayer can be an ongoing conversation with God (1 Thess 5:17), much like you might have with a good friend, a loving spouse, or an approachable parent. Only asking God for things in prayer can result in treating our heavenly father like a religious Santa Claus, thus making the relationship shallow and self-centered. Prayers of praise, prayers of thanksgiving, even prayers of confession or repentance, and vows, all have important spiritual functions which should not be neglected.

If prayers to God stem from an ongoing relationship, then that conversation should be rich and diverse, both spoken and silent, with varied attitudes, postures, and venues. All these factors and more can become very influential in enriching our spiritual lives.

Learning To Pray

Most of us were not formally taught how to pray, except perhaps for basics, like ending each request with "in the name of Jesus" or something similar. Most of us learned to pray by listening to those around us as we grew up: parents, other family members, teachers, pastors, or preachers, etc. Depending on which of those models had the most impact, we may have a rich prayer life or something much less if we only remember standard phrases repeated often in our youth. Many remember the Lord's Prayer (Matt 6: 9-13), which can be recited privately or in groups. Other biblical examples of prayer are diverse in purpose, types, places, times, postures, and attitudes.

Types of Prayer

In terms of their purpose and function, we can identify seven basic types.

1. **Petitions**: such prayers ask God for something for ourselves.
2. **Intercessions**: these prayers ask God to do something for someone else, imploring God on their behalf.
3. **Praises**: we glorify or exalt God for his character, creation, or salvation, etc.
4. **Thanksgiving**: we thank God for something he has done, usually for the one praying (or his family or people). Often, prayers of praise and prayers of thanksgiving overlap.
5. **Confession and Repentance**: these types of prayer are where we come to God and confess our sin(s) and then vow to repent or change and do better.
6. **Blessing**: a blessing can ask God to bless someone else, to bless ourselves, or even for God himself to be blessed.
7. **Vow**: such rare prayers promise God something: "I will give half of all I make next month to the poor," or "I will skip lunch and spend that time praying for others next week," and so on because of something the petitioner asks God to grant. These prayers are often coupled with confession and repentance.

Places, Times, & Postures

The Bible depicts many settings, times, and postures that accompany prayer. Of course, we can pray any time and any place, but we might not always think about our posture. Further, there are certain times and places we might not consider appropriate for talking to God.

Places. God will hear us anywhere we pray, but ancient people often saw certain places as especially appropriate in Scripture. Examples include Mount Sinai where Moses received the Ten Commandments; where the old Temple had existed (the Temple Mount, as it is known today); and when Jesus withdrew to Gethsemane. For us today, it might be a location where God did something special, or a gravesite, or at home. Some people designate a special place in the home, yard, or garden for their prayer life to help set apart that place for God.

Times. Certain events were always accompanied by prayer: the Sabbath, worship services, but also the agricultural seasons essential in the ancient world. Today, we might not be aware of planting or harvesting seasons, but we have New Year's Day, Thanksgiving, Christmas, and other holidays where prayer might be important. Births, birthdays, weddings, anniversaries, funerals, and other common life events are significant milestones when prayers can be offered. Some people like to set a specific time of prayer: when they first awake, or at sundown, for example. Despite all these instances of prayer connected to special events, our most important prayers can come in our normal, daily life.

Postures. Today we do not often pray like people in the Bible and ancient times. Certain postures regularly went along with certain types of prayer.

Petitions and intercessions were offered with hands out, palms upraised (e.g., Exod 9:29; Job 11:13; Ps 63:4; 1 Tim 2:8). Prayers of confession or repentance might be offered on one's knees or even face down, as before a king (e.g., 1 Kgs 8:54; Ezra 9:5-6; Eph 3:14-19). Standing with arms up was common when offering praises to God. These postures are another way to enrich our prayers beyond merely bowing our heads, by far the most common trait today.

The places, times, and postures of prayer can be private or public. Public or corporate prayer involves someone (or several people) leading a prayer for everyone in attendance. This is obviously in contrast with praying alone, in private. (Sometimes, you might pray in private, but with another person or two.) Both settings for prayer can have different purposes, but still involve some aspect of spiritual growth, worship, or service. Because a Christian does not stand alone—each of us should be part of a community of faith—we depend on our brothers and sisters for encouragement and accountability which both can involve prayer. In community, we can also worship and serve others together. Typically, corporate prayer has more to do with broader issues such as our faith community, the church universal, or political leaders, etc. In private, we more often ask God for something for ourselves, or discuss matters of a more personal nature, not always appropriate for public settings.

FASTING

The Bible often mentions fasting, though we hear less about it among modern people of faith. People fasted alone or with others, often connected with a prayer of lament or an intercession of extreme importance (e.g., Judg 20:26; Ezra 8:23; Dan 9:3). Jesus fasted (Matt 4:2), and expected his followers to do so (Matt 6:16), but also suggested that his disciples did not need to do so until he returned to heaven (Mark 2:18–20). If Jesus expected his disciples to fast, we probably should.

Simply put, fasting is going without a meal or more than one meal. But it is not just going without food; that is just being hungry or dieting. Spiritual fasting means sacrificing your meal time to do something else, such as prayer, study, or service. It can also remind us of our dependence on God for food, the need to fuel our bodies that God has created.

When we fast and pray, we may follow several biblical examples. Fasting can go along with many of the categories of prayer discussed above. David interceded for his son while fasting (2 Sam 12:16). Ezra 8:23 implies that fasting strengthens prayers. Confessions are commonly associated with fasting. That is what the people of Israel did (1 Sam 7:6). Daniel did so on behalf of Israel (9:3–5). Jonah convinced the Ninevites to do so (Jonah 3:5-10). With prayer and fasting, Paul and Barnabas appointed elders (Acts 14:23).

Jesus encouraged his followers not to let anyone know that they are fasting (Matt 6:17-18). Similarly, our attitude in prayer is important, according to Jesus, where any kind of personal pride or boasting is inappropriate (Luke 18:9-14).

You can begin a fast in simple ways such as perhaps skipping lunch to spend time in study, meditation, or prayer. You could extend that to a 24-hour period. Some go longer, but it is important to understand how your body works so that you do not endanger your health. The length of time is less important than the attitude and the practice behind it.

Healthcare professionals should be consulted before extensive fasting. Some people might be severely hypoglycemic and could not go too long without food. In such cases, giving up a certain kind of food would be easier to do for long periods of time.

In summary, fasting gives believers a countercultural way to strengthen faith and can help us focus our prayers as well as remind us of our utter dependence on God for all our blessings.

WORSHIP

The simplest definition of worship is the veneration or praise of God. Since God is the Creator of the universe and sustainer of all life, it is through him that we find meaning, therefore he should be praised. The beginning of the Lord's Prayer is a good example of worshiping God for who he is:

Our Father in heaven,
May your holy name be honored.
May your kingdom come,
May your will be done,
On earth as it is in heaven.

(After these opening words, notice how the rest of the prayer turns to requests that God provide us with sustenance, forgiveness, and help us avoid temptation.)

Give us today the food we need.
Forgive us the wrongs we have done,
as we forgive the wrongs that others have done to us.
Do not bring us to hard testing,
but keep us safe from the Evil One. (Matt 6:11-13, GNT)

Worship can include other elements: thanksgiving, singing, music, prayers, sermons or exhortations, fellowship, silence—many of the other disciplines discussed earlier.

God should be the primary focus, the main emphasis of our public worship, what we do within our faith community. We might think of a building with rows of seats facing forward toward a pulpit. Someone often stands to offer a prayer, or some other liturgical act. But that is only *one* way of worshiping God. Worship could also be a time where believers gather to sing and offer prayers of praise, or a time of silence to contemplate the love and compassion of God.

Worship can also be done alone. You can sit in a room, or perhaps better, outside somewhere, and recite one of the creation Psalms, or offer a prayer praising God for who he is and his acts throughout history. As long as God is the focus, and your attention is directed toward lifting up God's name in praise or adoration, you are worshiping him.

SERVICE

Being a follower of Jesus means more than just going to church and religiously practicing spiritual disciplines; it means serving others—both believers and unbelievers. Why? The concept of service permeates the New Testament and Jesus came to serve (Mark 10:45). If we seek to follow Jesus, we also must serve. Also, believers are God's ambassadors (2 Cor 5:20)—part of his presence on earth. Some churchgoers in the evangelical community think that their purpose is merely spreading the good news about Jesus. But telling people about the gospel is not the only way to spread it. Loving actions speak louder than doctrine alone.

How did Jesus serve (Mark 10:45)? He provided people with spiritual encouragement and compassion, but also helped them with their physical needs. Jesus was deeply moved by how difficult life can be. He stood with his disciples on a nearby mountain beside Jerusalem and wept over the physical, mental, and emotional troubles people would encounter (Luke 19:41).

If we are to follow Jesus, we should also lovingly serve others. There are so many ways to serve others, both directly and indirectly. You can serve at food kitchens, donate clothes to the poor, visit shut-ins, hospitals, or retirement homes. Sometimes just being there with hurting people means more than you might imagine to those without family members who care.

Jesus went much further than any of us could hope to do: he offered his life as a sacrifice for others. Few of us will ever be called upon to give up our lives, but we can find ways to make personal sacrifices so that others might have what they need. We might commonly think this means giving of our money or goods, which is worthwhile, but it can also mean giving of our time so that others will benefit. For it to be a true sacrifice, of course, it must cost you something. While giving a few dollars to a worthy cause serves others, if it does not cause you to suffer in some way, or miss out on some benefit that you would otherwise enjoy, it is not a sacrifice. Think about ways you can give up something so that someone else benefits. Another practice might be to find ways to anonymously help someone (Matt 6:1). This removes the opportunity for you to receive thanks for what you did—

a type of reward. To be genuinely offered, sacrificial service to others should not come with rewards or accolades.

Since Jesus himself served the physical and spiritual needs of both believers and unbelievers, the early church did the same. However, Scripture prioritizes providing support to other believers, the family of God, as is described more fully in Chapter 7, "Loving Others."

FELLOWSHIP

Being with other believers remains a crucial part of our spiritual journey with God. The concept of a faith community is found throughout Scripture from beginning to end. From the early Hebrews, to the times of judges and kings, to the exile of Israel, to the return to Jerusalem and their lands, and throughout the Roman occupation, the Jewish people are often discussed as a community that needed each other throughout life as God's covenant people.

It is the same after the coming of Jesus and the development of his church. While believers met in the temple and synagogues for religious purposes, those words did not refer to the people themselves. In the New Testament, the word translated "church" referred to people called out from the world to worship God, not a place where they met, which is often what it means to people today.

6. Loving God

God did not create us to act solely as individuals. In our faith, we need each other for support, encouragement, and accountability, and sometimes even for our material needs. As Paul the Apostle writes, the church can do God's work better as a group because some of us plant and others water, but God "makes things grow" (1 Cor 3:5-9).

The value of community is sometimes difficult for us to understand because, while we know how isolation and loneliness can affect us negatively, we live in a culture that stresses individuality. It was not so in the ancient world. Family, tribe, and clan were crucial for survival and growth. Unlike today, it was very difficult and dangerous for a person to be alone for too long, but it was more than that: God created us to be a family. This is why early Christians called each other "brother" and "sister." Our spirituality is stunted if we do not live out our faith in community.

But a spiritual community can take many forms. We might think first of a typical church community in a neighborhood, where people from the town congregate. Yet it could also be a small group meeting in a home, a collection of devoted people, with each doing their part to follow Jesus. Some individuals withdrew for spiritual purposes. Moses, Elijah, David, Jesus, and Paul all did so at times, to focus on prayer, fasting, and study.

CONFESSION

Confession can be both a spiritual discipline in terms of its act (confessing your sins to another person) and a prayer (offering a prayer of confession to God). This may be one of the most difficult spiritual disciplines because we are not inclined to humble ourselves by admitting our sins, perhaps especially to another person. Some even avoid studying the various types of sin described in Scripture so they can avoid confronting themselves when they fall short. If we did not fail to live within our created purpose, there would be no need for confession. But because we need to be honest in our relationship with God, confession is necessary. All believers do fail to be what our creator God intended (Rom 3:23), so it is both necessary and spiritually healthy to admit that all of us need a Savior.

Except for sensitive issues best dealt with privately, when we confess to God, our family, friends, or some group, the main purpose is to face our situation head-on by naming specifics so we can deal with them. When we bring our sin out into the light and admit its power over us, we diminish that power. It is always difficult to change our behavior even after confession, but repentance is almost impossible when we ignore our need to follow Jesus more closely.

Without the intent to do better, confession becomes superficial. As we admit the ugliness of our sin, we need to disavow it. We might say something like, "This is not me nor who I want to be. I am sorry I failed you (God and/or others); I repent of it, and pledge to do better in the future." Those battling various addictions must rededicate themselves to abstinence to stay healthy which is an explicit type of repentance, a commitment to change.

There are many examples of confession (Lev 5:5, 16:21, 26:40; Num 5:7). God desires confession:

> If we confess our sins, he is faithful and just and will forgive us our sins and purify us from all unrighteousness. (1 John 1:9)

We all know that standing before God or others, and naming what we have done wrong, is difficult. Perhaps this is why we do not see or hear of public confessions too often in today's world. Even if we do admit something, we are often inclined to soften it with excuses or reasons: "I was so tired," or "he provoked me," and so on. It is not just politicians or corporate leaders who make excuses; most of us are very good at doing the same thing. Genuine confession should avoid excuses by simply saying: "I did wrong" or "I committed this sin." When dealing with an omniscient God, the best policy is not to try to dodge accountability or try to disguise the scope of our disobedience. He already knows the thoughts and intentions of our heart.

If your sin was public, then the confession should be public. If it hurt one person, it should be before them (see Jas 5:16). But sin is always an affront to

God, so it is always appropriate to pray our confessions to God (whether in public or in private).

Sometimes, if a group of people has acted against God's ways, a leader can offer a prayer of confession for all the people. Ezra commanded that prayers of confession be offered for all those who married foreign wives (Ezra 10:11-14). Sometimes, all the people together offer a prayer of confession (see Neh 9:3).

What should a confession look like? It can be a simple statement, such as Psalms 32:5, where David acknowledged (did not cover up) his sin and then received forgiveness.

Nehemiah's public confession, for all the people, is more developed:

> I confess the sins we Israelites, including myself and my father's house, have committed against you. We have acted very wickedly toward you. We have not obeyed the commands, decrees and laws you gave your servant Moses. (Neh 1:6-7)

Notice how there are no excuses, no reasons, no defenses. Pure humility is the goal.

David's confession in Psalm 51 is an excellent structure to use for our own prayers. Briefly, he committed adultery with Bathsheba and then had her husband killed in battle. He begins by asking God for mercy (vv1-2), followed by the confession itself (v3). David then states that he understands the damage he has done to others and the hurt he has caused God, acknowledging that God would be justified in punishing him (v4). Following his confession, he appeals to God to forgive him (vv7-12). David closes the prayer with a pledge of repentance for the future (vv13-17). In such prayers, we cast ourselves on the ground before God and others, asking for mercy and forgiveness after genuinely confessing what we have done wrong, without excuse or reasons. We acknowledge we have hurt God and others, and know that it is God who forgives.

SILENCE

Silence can also be part of prayer, worship, or even service. Listening is as important as talking. The common biblical phrase, "wait for the Lord," is a good concept to think about and practice.

> But those who are waiting for the Lord will have new strength; they will get wings like eagles: running, they will not be tired, and walking, they will have no weariness. (Isa 40:31, Basic Bible in English).

This concept of waiting for the Lord appears throughout Scripture in different contexts (Num 9:8, Ps 130:5, Prov 8:34, Rom 8:25). Believers should practice patience as a sign of trusting God.

Most of us live in such a busy, noisy world, that taking time for silence is beneficial. When you slow down, and try to quiet your mind, it becomes much more feasible to meditate.

Find a place where you will not be disturbed or interrupted. Remove all distractions, as much as you can, especially technology. Sit or kneel comfortably. After a session of prayer, sit in silence for five or ten minutes—longer if you can. Sometimes this can take practice, because many of us are not used to just *sitting* quietly. You will find your mind wanders—that is okay, we simply want to bring it back to silence and stillness. After practicing silence in prayer for a time, people often report feeling more self-aware, less anxious, and more connected to God and his purposes.

MOVING FORWARD

If we want to draw closer to God (as the foundation for following Jesus), to hear his voice more clearly, and to live a life worthy of him, the spiritual disciplines briefly described here can give Christ-followers a daily focus and form the basis to personally reap benefits that cannot be gained otherwise. While your experience will vary, help from other believers and those more mature in the faith should help you uncover deficiencies that can be remedied with dependence on God and help from the Holy Spirit.

There is, of course, the danger that those practicing spiritual disciplines begin to think that the mere practice of such routines shows or increases one's faith. Such a belief confuses rote religion with the spirituality desired by God. Despite the importance of sacrifices to Israel, for example, God did not want sacrifices without a humble heart. In that same sense for Christians, religious rituals and personal spirituality must work together to develop the godliness needed to become more like Jesus.

7.
Loving Others

The second Greatest Commandment is the basis for all godly, human relationships.

In World War II, Desmond T. Doss was a conscientious objector who believed in Jesus and risked his life on the battlefield to save others. As a combat medic, he refused to carry a weapon, and yet was awarded the Congressional Medal of Honor. Hollywood portrayed his heroism in the movie *Hacksaw Ridge*. While fellow soldiers harassed him during training, nobody questioned the depth of his faith when they saw his bravery under fire. After repeatedly risking his life to rescue the wounded on Okinawa and elsewhere, Doss earned the respect of any who doubted his courage. Although others did not share his beliefs, they knew that he took them seriously. "Greater love has no one than this, that he lay down his life for his friends" (John 15:13).

To follow Jesus as Lord and Master requires self-sacrifice as we take up our own cross (Matt 16:24). While few will be portrayed on film to demonstrate their response to God's word, all believers will have opportunities to make sacrifices. Responding to the second Greatest Commandment, "Love your neighbor as yourself" (Matt 22:39), can happen anywhere. Further, Jesus makes clear that we are to especially love our fellow believers. "A new command I give you: Love one another. As I have loved you, so you must love one another. By this all men will know that you are my disciples, if you love one another" (John 13:34-35).

RELATIONSHIPS DEVELOP OVER TIME

Those who follow Jesus relate to others based upon their primary relationship (loving God with all their heart, soul, strength, and mind). Spiritual maturity, like psychological maturity, takes time, and there are things that you can do to encourage as well as discourage it.

The developmental changes that take place in children from birth through puberty and beyond are numerous—some take place relatively quickly and some take place over a long period of time. Studies of Adverse Childhood Experiences (ACEs) demonstrate that traumatic events (death, divorce, physical or sexual abuse, poverty, neglect, etc.) before the age of 18 impact a person's development far beyond that age. Just like ACEs impair healthy growth, the same things can happen on one's spiritual journey. Without a stable, supportive environment that encourages healthy development, a dysfunctional religious family can stunt later spiritual growth. Studies by John Bradshaw and others about our family of origin affirm that concepts planted at an early age can dramatically influence child development.

Unlike child development, the path of spiritual growth cannot be measured as easily. A child's changes in height, weight, and certain motor skills track some aspects of maturation, but a follower of Jesus has no such metrics. This suggests the importance of spiritual mentors.

In a healthy Christian community, believers care enough to encourage, to comfort, and to hold each other accountable. This requires intimate relationships with those who share the values and goals of a common connection in Christ. Practicing spiritual disciplines helps us grow in our relationship with God, but growth is not something we can really monitor on our own. None of us see ourselves or hear ourselves as others do. Without trusted feedback, we are each somewhat blind and deaf. We need help from others who care about us so that we can spiritually grow.

The people around us impact our values, thinking, worldview, and more. Some who grew up in an evangelical church remember the phrase, "Bad company corrupts good morals" (1 Cor 15:33, NASB). Further, both our nature (genetics) and nurture (development) depend on our parents.

Relationships do not just shape each believer by teaching, encouragement, and accountability. They also help us discover how we each can best serve, so that all our individual talents and experiences

can be used in working for the kingdom. New believers are not only being taught how to grow in
Christ by watching the model of Christlike behavior in others, but also how to become an integral
part of the work of God in that same intimate
community.

All types of injuries need to heal. When injured in
an accident, our bodies need to heal. Believers who
are part of a spiritual body (Rom 12:4-8) can also
be hurt, both directly and indirectly, in ways that
keep them from serving God or others. Like a broken arm in a cast, believers broken by spiritual
damage can become immobile and thus atrophy
like the muscles that normally move a broken bone.
The injured parts often need rehabilitation before
they can function normally for the good of the
whole body. Few remove their own spiritual casts;
someone else must do it for them to begin the
process of rehabilitation, recovery, and renewal.
What some fail to appreciate is that the indirect
damage from bad religious habits, developed over
time, takes even longer to overcome. They must be
recognized for what they are: influences that do not
contribute toward spiritual growth. The rapport
needed to begin such developmental conversations
requires much more intimate and extended interactions than can typically occur during casual chats at
church.

DIFFERENT TYPES OF PEOPLE

The second Greatest Commandment is "Love your neighbor as yourself" (Matt 22:39). Since neighbors vary, biblical instructions help believers relate to different categories of people: more mature disciples, other believers/spiritual siblings, earthly family, secular neighbors, and enemies. This chapter's main emphasis will be on spiritual community, but any such grouping of people involves overlapping situations. For example, members of your earthly family can also be members of your spiritual family or even enemies, those who consciously try to harm you. Each of us usually functions in many different roles at the same time and must balance them all.

More Mature Disciples

It has sometimes been difficult for less mature believers to recognize and acknowledge their more mature spiritual leaders who should, but do not always, guide them in their growth. Some churchgoers have trouble accepting authority. Others have trouble accepting their own limits, their own tendencies toward a sinful nature (Gal 5:19-21), the degree to which they fall short of bearing "fruit of the spirit" (Gal 5:22-23), or how they fail to develop qualities that help them be effective and productive as they serve Jesus (2 Pet 1:5-8). So that believers understand why it is in their best interests to pay attention to the more mature among their spiritual community, let us briefly summarize some of the complex responsibilities of leadership that none ever fully master.

The best leaders (for *any* organization, not just religious ones) are those who see themselves as servant leaders. This is the model that Jesus taught and practiced himself, and the model urged by New Testament writers. Such leaders willingly sacrifice their own good for that of others, do their best to live by what they teach, do not think of themselves as better in any way, and are completely transparent in their work and goals. Trying to help others become more like Jesus, they encourage, equip, and admonish others. This servant-leader approach encourages relationships not hierarchy. While not all leaders can achieve such ideals, the best ones try.

Veteran servant leaders know that new believers can be fragile while struggling with things in their past and in their spiritual development. Most believers are trying to do their best, with the tools they have (some more than others) and the baggage they carry (some more than others).

Not just leaders, but any believer can help by sharing their experiences and encouraging others. Briefly, all individuals in a local spiritual community are responsible for every other spiritual sibling, whether new or mature, to assist in their growth. We are all our brethren's keepers.

Other Believers (Spiritual Siblings)

When asked about his family, Jesus said, "For whoever does the will of my Father in heaven is my brother and sister and mother" (Matt 12:50). While this might be understood by some as a shocking statement, Jesus emphasized the importance of spiritual ties—his father's kingdom—over earthly ties. Only in that sense does a spiritual family preempt the stated importance of an earthly family and its multiple, intergenerational relationships which all still matter.

The words "brother" and "sister" might have lost some of their meaning in today's blended families, but the New Testament extensively uses them. The most common term, "brother," refers to fellow believers as a whole. In the singular it refers to men (over 100 times), in the plural (over 100 times) it means both men and women. Believers can think of Jesus as our elder brother. The term "sister" (used over 20 times) refers specifically to women believers.

The use of these terms means even more when placed in their original context. Soldiers in the Roman military often called each other "brother." People of the same ethnicity or those who had Roman citizenship might do so as well, though examples are rare. There is some evidence that adherents of Epicurean philosophy used those terms, but a group of disparate people, from every social status, ethnicity, age, and family—Romans, Greeks, bar-

barians, slaves, and free—would never have used these terms for each other in that culture. Yet the early Christians understood their diverse group as a family created in Christ by God through the cross. Even other religious groups, whether it was the Roman or Greek gods and goddesses, or the mystery religions, did not use those intimate terms. It is no wonder that many in that world were scandalized by early Christian groups and their definition of a spiritual family. Such an egalitarian approach to relationships flew in the face of normal social hierarchies.

Many biblical passages tell us that our heavenly father sees those in Christ as part of God's own family. This model for God's children is a nurturing group of people who seek the best for each other and for the whole. They act out of selfless *agape* love, not from any personal agenda. The use of family language to describe God's collection of believers is no accident. Such people depend on a shared intimacy, not often found elsewhere in society—especially in today's culture.

Their spiritual bond binds them together because they share a common purpose of trying to become more like Jesus. Living their lives focused on *agape* love sets them apart from most secular people who have other motivational priorities, usually involving self-interest.

The most common New Testament refrain is for believers to "love one another," a phrase often repeated alone or in context with other clear guidance. Furthermore, such love is how "all men" will know that we are his disciples (John 13:35). Many verses echo the mandate to love the brethren (John 13:34; Rom 13:8; 1 Peter 1:22; 1 John 3:11, 23, 4:7, 12).

What such love entails is outlined in other verses that direct believers to "be devoted" (Rom 12:10); "live in harmony" (Rom 12:16); not judge or hinder other believers (Rom 14:13); "accept" (Rom 15:7); "instruct" (Rom 15:14); "agree with" (1 Cor 1:10); "serve" (Gal 5:13); "be patient" (Eph 4:2); forgive "just as in Christ God forgave you" (Eph 4:32); "submit" (Eph 5:21); "offer hospitality" (1 Pet 4:9); and "encourage one another" (1 Thess 5:11; Heb 3:13, 10:25).

We are to "share with God's people who are in need" (Rom 12:13). Jesus' brother makes a similar statement about helping "a brother or sister" (Jas 2:15-16). When helping those in need, "believers" get priority (Gal 6:10). Such sharing began in the early church (Acts 2:44-45).

Confrontations among a spiritual family cannot always be avoided (Matt 18:15-17). Where conflicts about sin must be resolved with help from a third party (because of a lack of response by an immature believer), it should still be done with compassion and firmness. The theology behind this is that (1) God has blessed mature leaders with the ability to help resolve conflict when it is necessary and (2) in a Christian community, the actions of every believer directly or indirectly impact the whole body. Clear, repeated disobedience to Scripture can negatively influence a spiritual body just as biological diseases can infect our entire physical body.

Continued stubbornness and a refusal to listen to or to submit to those exercising authority over their own community can result in sanctions. Such a tragic occurrence should be rare, but might be necessary once all other avenues have been exhausted (see Matt 18:17). As Paul explains in one of the few areas considering this topic (1 Cor 5:9-13), this approach is not intended to sanction unbelievers, but rather, only those who view Jesus as God's son and the Bible as authoritative.

When churches lose sight of their purpose, new converts can become organizational orphans, left without spiritual parents to guide them through the trials and tribulations of spiritual growth. Like young children without adult guidance, they can be influenced by those only slightly more mature, resulting in stunted development during key phases of life. Just as secular growth in the absence of engaged parents will be stunted by society's major influencers (Madison Avenue, Hollywood, Silicon Valley, and peer groups), spiritual status can hinge on similar factors.

Earthly Family

Everyone has some type of family unit which entails basic responsibilities as a child, parent, brother, or sister and so on. While we cannot pick our earthly family who greatly influences our developing thoughts on life, including those about religion and spirituality, we can pick our spouse, a very important choice.

Marriage matters because Paul writes that believers should not be "unequally yoked" with unbelievers (2 Cor 6:14). That phrase refers to the practice of connecting two oxen together, side-by-side, with a harness and a wooden bar, pulling a cart. If one of the oxen is weaker than the other, they are "unequally yoked," and the wagon will not move properly or might even tip over. Paul applies this analogy to believers. Even if a believer is strong, being connected so closely to an unbeliever will cause the stronger one to veer to the side and maybe wobble.

If you are a strong believer, you might be tempted to think that a weak spouse cannot affect you—that instead you will affect them. But as the analogy about not being unequally yoked suggests, when tied together, the weaker can affect the stronger. The Hebrew Bible's prohibition against intermarriage with those who serve foreign gods makes a similar point.

Paul's discussion about being unequally yoked can apply to any close association where each person affects the other. This does not mean that we should not mingle with unbelievers. Jesus interacted with people of all sorts of backgrounds, and was criticized for it. But believers should be careful whom they allow to influence their daily lives and their developing spiritual maturity.

While our priority as believers is to help our own church family, as discussed earlier, some boundaries exist. "If anyone does not provide for his relatives, and especially for his immediate family, he has denied the faith and is worse than an unbeliever" (1 Tim 5:8). Balance is vital.

Some say that Jesus made harsh statements (Luke 14:26) when he spoke about his followers hating their own family. But he then says that his disciples must even hate their "own life." Such a statement outlines how a believer must set aside earthly priorities for the cause of Christ. The next verse says, "Anyone who does not carry his cross and follow me cannot be my disciple."

Secular Neighbors

The world does not share the same values as those who try their best to follow Jesus. Thus, the New Testament speaks to those who would follow God's son. Those who do not believe, obviously, do not share a believer's views on how to live a life in sacrificial service to others.

Cultural influences often go against God's created purpose. People can lead us astray in subtle ways—especially if their commonly accepted views are at odds with Christ. Throughout history, as well as today, some Christians responded by withdrawing or isolating themselves from anything deemed ungodly. This is not what we are called to do. Christians are called to be "in the world, but not of the world" (implied in John 17:15-16; Rom 12:2; Jas 1:27b). After all, we cannot be God's ambassadors (2 Cor 5:20) if we are not around unbelievers, but we should still take care where and when we make long-term personal connections. Finally, we never know when we might encounter someone in need, like the "Good Samaritan" did (Luke 10:25-37).

Enemies

What makes following Christ different from many other religions are his directions to "love your enemies" (Matt 5:44), "do good to those who hate you" (Luke 6:27), and "bless those who persecute you; bless and do not curse" (Rom 12:14). "In fact, everyone who wants to live a godly life in Christ Jesus will be persecuted" (2 Tim 3:12). Thus, we should expect enemies, but we are not supposed to repay evil with evil because vengeance is up to God (Rom 12:17-19).

Still, believers who become politically active can expect secular pushback from those who oppose religious activists trying to shape public policy in the name of God. Such a reaction is not the same as persecution directed at those trying to exercise their freedom of religion. Those who engage in partisan politics enter a warlike free-for-all where anything goes. Chapter 10 discusses many aspects of involvement in the political arena by believers or their leaders.

Some religious behaviors, of course, have earned public condemnation. High profile scandals, theologically borderline doctrines, ungodly actions ostensibly based on Scripture, and con artists who take advantage of vulnerable churchgoers, have predictably resulted in outrage.

Churchgoers are no longer as respected as they once were in our increasingly post-Christian society. So, while living out our faith will always make some enemies, maybe that persecution will have the result it had long ago and help sincere Christ-followers reaffirm their faith in God.

TREATING UNBELIEVERS LIKE BELIEVERS

As ambassadors for Christ (2 Cor 5:20), of course, believers should always be ready to discuss their faith (1 Pet 3:15) as well as graciously respond to unbelievers (Col 4:5-6).

To expect unbelievers to act like believers is not logical because they have their own, self-determined set of values. Even if unbelievers lived their lives according to so-called Christian values, they would still lack a basic relationship with God. One role of the church is to bring unbelievers to belief in Christ (John 20:31). Only then are churches to make assessments of those who accept biblical authority as members of its spiritual community of believers (1 Cor 5: 9-13).

Scripture indicates that all people will be accountable for their actions, not just the religious. But, while unbelievers will be judged and found wanting, that is God's role, not ours. My focus here is upon helping believers understand a more spiritual response to their Lord and Master.

OUR CHALLENGES

The challenge for believers remains two-fold: love God and love others. Taken together these two commandments comprehensively summarize what matters most to our heavenly father.

Having leaders that help guide each believer toward spiritual maturity remains essential, but nothing can take the place of loving encouragement or feedback provided by spiritual siblings.

Why keep discussing this? There are many reasons, but my focus is on the spiritual growth of each individual Christian. We will all face what the Bible refers to as Judgment Day (discussed in chapter 8). What that entails is shadowed in mystery, but we do know that we will all be held accountable. In one sense, it will not matter where we worshiped or which doctrines we believed. What will matter is our own attitudes and actions, our relationships with God and others, how we responded to what Jesus affirmed as the two Greatest Commandments.

Moving Forward

The ability for Christ-followers to love all their neighbors, even enemies, depends on their own spiritual community's broader focus on helping each individual Christian's maturation. Thus, each believer's first and most important obligation is to spiritual siblings, to those who share the same goal of submission to God. While each of us bears a responsibility to love God with all our heart, soul, strength, and mind, we should not be alone in this endeavor. We each need help.

Spiritual communities should be welcoming to nonbelievers as well as believers. As society becomes more isolated and has fewer intimate relationships, a tight-knit community of like-minded Christ-followers may become attractive to unbelievers, but is also crucial to its own health.

Group intimacy depends on size. It is an unfortunate irony that it is easier to feel alone in a large group of churchgoers than it is to feel alone in a small group where every person is affirmed. Congregational gatherings have their purpose, but small groups remain essential to intimacy.

The dynamic nature of all relationships suggests that they be revisited periodically to see how well they are going. That is a core function of spiritually intimate communities of believers who look after one another. We are our brothers' and sisters' keepers, but we need mature leaders.

The best servant leaders will, among other things, help us reflect on our relationships with others. But leaders face challenges in helping others if they have been neglecting their own status. All servants, especially leaders, need healthy self-care to avoid burnout which can be devastating.

While good leaders point people in the right direction, some of them fail to recognize that each believer's journey can greatly vary. Paul writes that he has finished the race—he does not say he won the race (2 Tim 4:7). Paul stayed faithful, always trying to grow, despite his setbacks. Similarly, many competitive athletes always strive to do their personal best, even if they do not win.

When another believer is in crisis, it will really help to have previously established an intimate rapport. Few people find comfort in difficult times from someone who does not know them or their personal situation. Core relationships must be developed over time, not on the spur of the moment.

Unbelieving neighbors do not need to be confronted about ungodly behavior as if they were believers, because they do not subscribe to godly values. That does not mean that believers should not be social with outsiders, but such relationships will be different than those with spiritual siblings.

8.
More Like Jesus

To become more like Jesus, disciples need to seriously focus on that lifelong goal.

Scripture portrays Jesus as someone to follow and Satan as God's adversary, the father of lies. Over the years several writers have outlined this classic conflict between good and evil.

While Southeast Alaska's natural beauty attracts both regular and celebrity tourists to Juneau, my favorite high-profile visitor remains Aleksandr Solzhenitsyn (1918-2008). Accompanied by a Russian Orthodox priest, this 1970 Nobel Laureate walked through our State Office Building's 8th floor atrium in May of 1975. Some employees heard he was in town, so we watched from upper levels. This literary icon had earlier expressed a universal idea that applies to each of us when he said, "The line dividing good and evil cuts through the heart of every human being."

Years earlier, George Bernard Shaw (1856-1950) explained a comparable indigenous concept:

"A Native American elder once described his own inner struggles in this manner: Inside of me, there are two dogs. One of the dogs is mean and evil. The other dog is good. The mean dog fights the good dog all the time. When asked which dog wins, he reflected for a moment and replied, 'the one I feed the most.'"

More recently, Pope Francis also said, "the boundary between good and evil runs through the heart of each of us." Similar admonitions occur throughout the wisdom literature of the Hebrew Bible while the Apostle Paul described his own struggles with good and evil (Rom 7:15-25).

KEEP YOUR EYES ON JESUS:
DO NOT BE DISTRACTED

At one conference I heard a Black minister speak about integrating a Christian college deep in America's Bible Belt. After the lecture, I asked him privately how he endured the racist abuse he had described. He said, "I try to keep my eyes on Jesus." I cannot improve upon that approach—the key to being an authentic, lifelong believer is keeping your eyes on Jesus (Heb 12:2).

Nobody, of course, ever wants to think they are wrong about God or doing what the Bible says. Further, some church leaders who intentionally mislead others are like "wolves in sheep's clothing"

(Matt 7:15; Acts 20:29) who can appear religious. Paul tells the church in Corinth that one of Satan's tactics is to disguise himself (2 Cor 11:14). After all, if a leader came to your church and said, "I am a disciple of Satan come to lead you astray," few would follow. But if they present themselves as an "angel of light" with an appealing message that sounds good, any of us might be fooled. That is also why it is important to learn how to search Scripture (Acts 17:11) and not be deceived or distracted by God's adversary.

Jesus warned his followers about false teachers and false prophets—religious leaders who led people astray (Matt 24:4–13). Likewise, Paul met with the elders of the church in Ephesus and told them that some men would arise among them and "distort the truth in order to draw away disciples" (Acts 20:30). Sadly, sometimes leaders ignore God's main messages.

Whether they are leaders or not, all followers of Christ face temptations. Such enticements are often not right out in the open, where it is obvious that we are being tempted. Some dangers lurk in darkness, subtly attractive, or around corners, just waiting. In any case, if temptations were all terrible and obvious, few would have problems resisting them. We should have compassion for leaders who succumb to temptations, and pray for them, just as we pray for all believers who sin.

It is important for us to understand as believers who are tempted that Jesus also knows what it is like to be tempted. He can sympathize with us, comfort us, and give us strength—because he has been there and came through victoriously. The Son of Man knows what it is to be human.

From the beginning Satan has tried to get everyone to reject God. Unbelievers and nominal churchgoers are already in his grasp, so his primary targets are those who are learning to follow Jesus. New converts can easily fall prey to Satan's attacks. Church leaders who fail to encourage, facilitate, and monitor spiritual growth indirectly assist God's enemy. Jesus warns shepherds who fail to protect their sheep (who wander away) that they will be accountable (Matt 18:12-14).

KEEP YOUR HEAD & HEART ON CHRIST'S MESSAGES

Modern church history contains many examples of "new and improved" versions of Christianity. Many religious organizations and their practices gradually tend towards rote actions and rituals that can become lifeless and need renewal. Eventually, someone notices. New ideas are not necessarily bad, especially when such approaches take a fresh look back at Scripture and the early church. We can criticize the Roman Catholic Church, or its ancient cousin the Eastern Orthodox Church, for their ritualized legacy, but meanwhile, most others have continued to splinter into pieces all over the theological map. Hundreds of denominations, sects, or even cults now exist, presumably to remedy some problems with existing churches. My tentative conclusion is that applied faith will always be a messy undertaking; no church will be without its flaws.

For readers unhappy with my criticism of any church, the late Dallas Willard mentioned that "disappointment" books form a "subcategory of Christian publishing." Several dozen in my personal library comment about what those authors see as wrong with some aspect of Christianity. They sometimes see tentative solutions on their analytical horizon, so I am hardly alone in my approach or in my suggestion that some things need serious attention.

As with many other aspects of American life, we value being able to choose. This can result in church shopping—seeking a group where you feel comfortable. While this may be desirable on some level, comfort should not be the point of those trying to follow Jesus. Rather, the goal should be to associate with a group of believers whose head and heart both connect in vertical and horizontal ways to help every believer. It may be in your best spiritual interest to look elsewhere if your church leaders are not helping you.

Religious groups like to emphasize the correctness of their sectarian doctrines or beliefs. No group, naturally, says that their views are wrong. But what is most important is each believer's response to the commands, teachings, and example of Jesus which provide constant challenges.

There are many things that an individual believer can do to follow Jesus, preferably in concert with the leadership of the church and other believers. To keep from getting lost, which can happen in various ways, we can look back at "the Way:" the principles and practices that Jesus left for his disciples to follow. Believers should bloom "where they are planted." See how God can use you wherever you find yourself; stop trying to seek something better unless necessary.

For American Christians, our frontier heritage gives us the tendency to try to pull ourselves up by our own bootstraps, to self-help ourselves into spiritual growth. But real growth comes by being connected to the Vine, Jesus Christ. This often requires help because none can see ourselves as others see us, how far we may have strayed. Revisit Paul's fruit of the Spirit (Gal 5:22-23) and Peter's building blocks of faith (2 Pet 1:5-12). Gauge these traits in your own life.

If you do not see some growth, if you keep repeating the same sins, it is important to seek help from trusted advisors, ones who love you and want to see you develop spiritually. But taking personal inventory requires sensitive insight and courage. We often cling to the past, unable to distinguish between whether we were taught to be churchgoers or Christ-followers.

If this is your struggle, you are not alone. Do not be too hard on yourself for being where you are. Most people do the best they can with the tools they have and the baggage they carry. As children, before we grew up, we depended on our parents to take care of our needs. As we often learn later in life, we often also need to lean on others for spiritual development. Sometimes only then can we identify missed opportunities or poor choices made in the past by ourselves and others. All life experiences offer lessons on several levels. Until and unless we learn from some types of mistakes, we are condemned to repeat the same ones and Jesus just might get lost.

REREADING THE GOSPELS

Since our call is to follow Jesus, periodically revisit his words and examples. Consider what he did, whom he spent time with (and why), whom he got angry with (and why), whom he healed, forgave, and encouraged (and why). Make sure to look at all the words of Jesus. What did he talk about most? What issues did he emphasize? Scripture provides ample perspectives.

A word of warning: it is often easy for believers and church organizations to get caught up in minutia and exclusively focus on certain biblical passages. They might argue about things that are not the core of faith. Jesus said that some things are more important than others, using the analogy of straining out gnats while swallowing camels (Matt 23:24).

Paul's letters echo Christ's instruction when he writes to avoid "foolish and stupid arguments" and "unprofitable and useless" quarrels (Phil 2:14, 2 Tim 2:23-26, and Tit 3:9-11). Do not get caught up with minor controversies that can never be settled. No believer perfectly practices their faith, which is a much more important goal than spending time trying to develop perfect beliefs.

CULTIVATING SPIRITUAL INTIMACY

Just knowing about Jesus is only the beginning. The goal of authentic discipleship is an ongoing relationship with God. The failure to pursue it is a pivotal reason why many Christians are not anything like Jesus. No simple phrase can capture what it means to live for Jesus, but it will always include a combination of both spiritual disciplines and daily decisions. Encouragement from spiritual siblings to love and good works and help from the Holy Spirit greatly contribute.

The opposite of following Jesus can be summarized as yielding to Satan's agenda. Sin places God in a secondary role in favor of our personal desires and wants. Living in a way that goes against your created purpose will always cause problems and create damage, though it will often not be immediately obvious. Followers of Jesus should know this and be on the alert for how "missing the mark" might be subverting their faith or various godly relationships.

USE IT OR LOSE IT

Like muscles that atrophy when we do not use them, our spirituality can shrivel if we do not focus on our core beliefs and practices each day. Religious rituals can help, but following Jesus involves deliberate responses to life's most challenging events. In the practice of our faith, we come to better understand some of its foundation, what God has said. Until we authentically practice the more difficult aspects of loving others, that belief remains largely academic.

If someone who confessed Christ long ago has not done a spiritual inventory lately, chances are they need a check-up by having someone they trust help them seriously evaluate their personal development. Like the warning signs of any disease, spiritual maladies have symptoms, too. One of these indicators is sin, doing things you should not be doing. But sin also includes not doing things you should be doing, the sin of omission (Jas 4:17). If you find that you have fallen into some routine sin, which is sometimes easy to overlook, you need to reconsider your spiritual life with God. Like your medical health, your spiritual health also involves ongoing self-care.

PARENTS REALLY MATTER

At a time in modern America when several factors shape young lives, each believing parent's emphasis needs to be on the spiritual development of themselves and of those closest to them, their children. Besides the influence of peer groups, Madison Avenue (advertising), Hollywood (movies & TV), Silicon Valley (internet, smartphones, & gaming) all now combine to impact the vulnerable young.

With limited life experience, it is difficult for children to assess the Christian faith or abstract concepts such as loving God, sacrifice for others, or atonement. If their learning about God never goes deeper as they age, their spiritual life will consist mainly of simplistic beliefs and practices.

If children never see their parents behave as if they were following Jesus outside of sacred rituals in a church building, those children will likely have no concept of what it means to follow Jesus. All such people only know what it means to go to church, an impression that tends to persist.

If hell scared you when young, if avoiding hell drove your conversion rather than a basic understanding of God's grace and love, that is a very limited view of Christianity. Such an approach treats Jesus as mainly a Savior, not your Lord and Master, someone who guides your life from conversion onward. While fear motivates on a visceral level, especially for the very young, being afraid loses its impact when children become teens. As young adults, they reassess all they have been told, and often discard what they have not seen in practice. Their experience at home helps them decide if their parents are mere churchgoers or authentic Christ-followers doing their best to become more like Jesus.

Unless Christianity's lessons find their way home to be discussed and applied in each family's life, such parents have largely abdicated their spiritual responsibilities to what happens at church.

Parents really matter. Based on a massive 2003–2005 research project entitled the National Study of Youth and Religion, author Kenda Creasy Dean writes at the very beginning of her 2010 book *Almost Christian: What the Faith of Our Teenagers Is Telling the American Church,* "…the religiosity of American teenagers must be read primarily as a reflection on their parents' religious devotion (or lack thereof) and, by extension, that of their congregations."

The main title of her book combines Acts 26:28 with what two 18th century preachers said plagued the church: it was "almost Christian." When parents depend on the church to instill an abiding religious faith in their children without demonstrating their own faith at home, their children will not be fooled for long. Parents who do not live for Jesus at home have no reasonable expectation to believe that their children will learn anything different at church. Some churchgoers may appear fine to their religious leaders, but will not fool their children about the nature or degree of their willingness to take up their own cross and live sacrificially.

JUDGMENT DAY

The fate of those who claim to be followers of Jesus will depend on what they did while on earth. That is not some legalistic calculation of their perfection—which no one can obtain in either belief or practice—it is rather their godly direction that matters. Were they making progress toward becoming more like their Lord and Master, their lifelong goal? That can only be assessed by a gracious God who knows the "thoughts and intentions" of each heart (Heb 4:12).

Regardless of their doctrinal purity, even the most self-centered churchgoer or religious zealot will at some point have to admit that they sometimes fall short of practicing what Jesus clearly preached. Christ's main message of *agape* love involves serious, authentic, and heart-felt concern for others— all out-of-touch with much of our current, narcissistic American society.

While many New Testament verses make clear that individuals will be accountable for their choices, two passages stand out. Matthew 7 provides broad guidance; chapter 25 gets specific.

In Matthew 7:21-29, Jesus warns that calling him Lord will not be enough if those who claim to be his followers do not also put his words into practice. Orthopraxy must follow orthodoxy.

The Son of Man will judge everyone from all nations by separating them into two groups (Matt 25:31–46). How we treat the "least of these"—the hungry or thirsty, strangers, the naked, the sick, prisoners—reflects how we, in effect, treat Jesus. However, the context is important.

Just before discussing sheep and goats, Jesus told the parable of the talents (Matt 25:14-30). Three servants were entrusted with different amounts of money. The two who used their talents to make more money were praised, "Well done, good and faithful servant! You have been faithful with a few things. I will put you in charge of many things! Come and share your master's happiness!" The servant who buried his money to protect it was not rewarded. In fact, he was called lazy and wicked, and was stripped of what he had been given. Not all of us have the same ability to serve God, but each of us has the responsibility to use what gifts we have. Do you use your talents or do you bury them? The daily practice of your faith is important to God.

Some churchgoers, knowingly or not, depend on their church to save them. They think that "my church is the right one and will make sure I am on the right path." But notice who is being evaluated in the above story about sheep and goats—it is individuals who are being judged—not their church. Your church may help you learn to follow Jesus— but then again, it might not.

Especially now, while many churches are desperate for new members, conflicts can emerge. Instead of helping churchgoers become Christ-followers, some churches try hard to attract new members.

Such churches even adopt customer-oriented marketing rather than teaching all that Jesus commands. Maybe your church focuses upon religion rather than on your spiritual growth. Maybe you are merely going to church rather than being faithful on your moment-by-moment journey to become more like Jesus. Maybe you need help to become a Christ-follower.

Rest assured that God will not be mocked, conned, or fooled, but on that last day, grace will abound from an all-knowing God who understands each person in depth. Unlike technicalities which can impair the insights of secular courts, our ultimate judge will not be limited in any way.

Moving Forward

As God in the flesh, Jesus should represent a life for all Christians to imitate. As our ultimate adversary, Satan represents evil, an ongoing threat to divert, distract, or deceive any who might try to become more like Jesus, and is thus a hindrance to any spiritual growth (Eph 6:11-18).

While discipleship begins at the change from unbelief to belief, it should continue to deepen as each new believer gets to know and be known by God's son. Those whom our Lord and Master does not know will not be acknowledged by him at Judgment (Matt 7:21-29). Church membership will not govern. What will matter is whether churchgoers have become Christ-followers who have been following Jesus by focusing on what he taught and modeled.

Keeping our eyes on Jesus remains the most basic goal for each believer. It becomes all too easy to slip into apathy by comparing ourselves to others rather than to the one who should stand out as our ultimate example, God's son. Meanwhile, our enemy, Satan, thrives when we take our eyes off Jesus, when we allow something or someone else to reign as our life's priority.

9.
The Great Omission

Some church leaders largely ignore the second and more important part of the Great Commission.

Having lived over 50 years in an Alaskan city without roads connecting it to the lower 48, I am a frequent flier when compared to most other Americans. While on planes, my seatmates would sometimes agree to politely discuss religion. When I discussed this book, a few offered their own thoughts. One man voiced a concern: was I just criticizing Christianity? "No," I replied. Like an internal auditor for any organization, I was looking for in-house solutions to our problems. He thanked me, said that it was long overdue, and wished me well. He had grown up in the church, but no longer attended, and was glad someone was serious about working on its many issues.

Little did this questioner know that dozens of books tackle the same issues: what is wrong with today's church. Based on personal insights, well-meaning authors offer constructive advice to fix what they see as broken. But I have not found many who focus on what I see as the evangelical church's biggest issue, what Dallas Willard (1935-2013) called "the great omission."

Emphasizing the first part of the Great Commission, making disciples, sometimes results in making mere converts rather than authentic followers. What easily gets ignored is the second, more important part of the apostolic mandate: teaching them to obey all that Jesus commanded (Matt 28:20). Immature converts who have not been taught how to do that will not be able to handle Satan's temptations amid the unavoidable struggles of life. It is an ongoing church problem if leaders do not recognize and take steps to remedy such ecclesiastical codependence (dysfunctional reliance upon clergy). Dependent churchgoers will eventually wither if they cannot stay connected to the Vine (John 15:1-6). Church leaders who do not shepherd their flock to follow Jesus are also stunted if they fail to help struggling believers. Leaders need to keep growing, too, and helping other believers contributes to their own growth.

If the point of being a Christian is to become more like Jesus—this book's major premise—then anything that gets in the way of that primary purpose needs to be carefully examined.

IMPORTANCE OF THE GREAT COMMISSION

Near the end of his earthly ministry, Jesus sent out his eleven closest followers on a mission:

Then Jesus came to them and said, "All authority in heaven and on earth has been given to me. Therefore, go and **make disciples** of all nations, baptizing them in the name of the Father and of the Son and of the Holy Spirit, and **teaching them to obey everything I have commanded you**. And surely, I am with you always, to the very end of the age." (Matt 28:18-20, emphasis added to distinguish between first and last part of this mandate)

We now call these missionaries "apostles" because they were "sent out," which is what the word means. What some today may not realize is that this mission dramatically expanded Christ's kingdom. After the Great Commission, not just Jews, but everyone, everywhere, could come to God. Why? The Greek word for nations referred to ethnic groups or peoples, not to be confused with modern political countries whose boundaries are often drawn without regard to ethnic subcultures.

The spiritual movement that became Christianity changed its focus. Jesus was first sent to "the lost sheep of Israel" (Matt 15:24). During his life, he told the Twelve to serve those same lost sheep (Matt 10:6), not the Gentiles or Samaritans (Matt 10:5). Long before, God promised "the father of the faithful" that his descendants would be blessed. Thus, Abraham became the father of many nations (Gen 17:4-7; see also Heb 8:7-13). Further, God promised that the whole world would be blessed through his descendants (Rom 4:16). Matthew's first chapter details the generations connecting Jesus, the son of David, to father Abraham. Thus, this Great Commission fulfills God's promise to bless all nations through Abram (Gen 12). But how does that happen?

Disciples learn to imitate or follow Jesus; the word "disciple" means "follower." If new converts never learn how to embody "everything" that Jesus commanded, but just go to church, that is a serious problem. If churchgoers fail to grasp the New Testament's clearest message about *agape* love, they have not become Christ-followers who take up their own cross in service to others. Why? The two Greatest Commandments about vertical love for God and horizontal love for others remain the core of everything that Jesus commanded his apostles to teach his disciples.

THE MISTAKE OF OVEREMPHASIZING EVANGELISM

For many, making converts is the primary goal of the Christian faith. Evangelism has been discussed globally, emphasized by high-profile media ministers, and taught from local pulpits. But has a new convert's spiritual journey been adequately outlined? Just as secular recruitment efforts sometimes fail to mention certain employment issues, should those being "sold" on Jesus also be told about the nature of taking up their own cross? Could it be that those selling Jesus as Savior sometimes forget to mention his role as Lord and Master?Three worldwide efforts in the last 50 years focused on evangelism: *The Lausanne Covenant* (1974), *The Manila Manifesto* (1989), and *The Cape Town Commitment: A Confession of Faith and Call to Action* (2010). Available on-line research contains extensive details about these efforts, but not about what happens to new believers after their conversion in response to those efforts. Why? What happens to new converts will depend on efforts of local congregations and their leaders to nurture those babes in Christ, to teach them how to become more like Jesus. How does that happen?

Without converts being taught that their faith involves more than going to church, their religion can easily become just one more event in a busy life. While the Great Commission is an imperative, the two Greatest Commandments are the foundation for its second part. Jesus said, "teaching them to obey everything that I have taught you" (Matt 28:20, NCV). Believers must be taught what it means to be a follower. Immature converts often cannot even take care of their own spirituality, let alone allow their lights to shine to glorify God.

Churchgoers themselves trying to make converts without knowing how to live as a disciple is like a salesperson working from scripted lines. People notice differences between someone's God-talk and life-walk. In a world saturated by marketing, salesmen who do not know their product in real life betray themselves as unpersuasive mouthpieces, persons not to be trusted. If Christians do not do their best to imitate Jesus, what does it say about the depth of their faith?

Failure to teach new believers about the fundamental role of *agape* love in Christ's messages is to misconstrue his entire ministry. To make converts without a subsequent emphasis on the need for spiritual maturity can easily lead to inadvertently creating shallow believers who fall away. From a logical standpoint, it makes little sense to focus on bringing new members in the front door, while at the same time allowing struggling old members to quietly slide out the back door.

God's message is not a product to be sold, but a way of life to adopt. It is a lifelong goal of becoming more like Jesus in thoughts, words, and actions. This process will always be a work-in-progress (even for the most mature) and requires mutual accountability relationships with other disciples.

Small groups are necessary to have intimate exchanges with spiritual siblings. To discern who is having trouble learning how to follow Jesus, a diagnosis needs to be specific. While pulpit sermons can impart biblical knowledge, they lack the ability to provide personalized feedback.

If new churchgoers only learn to parrot their church's talking points, instead of trying to follow Jesus, that becomes their standard—a low bar of faith. Those leaders who have grown up in such a church have probably not learned how to practice

God's two Greatest Commandments. Such leaders will likely become blind guides who are not trustworthy to guide others (Matt 23:16-26).

Some churches have no way to tell if their members are maturing except by noticing when someone has stopped attending. By then, it is usually too late. By the time many believers stop going to church, the accumulated resentment, boredom, or rejection is usually too much for their leaders to reverse, even if they tried. Some church leaders do not even follow up with those who leave, subtly implying that it is the churchgoer's fault for giving up. Like sheep that tend to wander away if not watched and cared for by their shepherd, new believers can do the same. Maybe that is why the Good Shepherd expressed concern about even one lost sheep (Matt 18:12-14).

Instead of paying attention to each individual's spiritual status, it is easy for church leaders to prioritize quantitative issues—things that can be counted—over qualitative matters, such as gauging each believer's ability to grapple with personal sin. One minister confided that his leadership only focused on attendance and contributions. In such a context, clergy must then determine how to fill their pews with more bodies, much like secular commerce explores how best to attract new customers. Sermons about taking up your own cross may not be popular.

THE TWO GREATEST COMMANDMENTS SUMMARIZE JESUS

Religious leaders asked God's son a key question, so his reply deserves careful review:

> Hearing that Jesus had silenced the Sadducees, the Pharisees came to him. One of them, an expert in the law, tested him with this question: "Teacher, which is the greatest commandment in the Law?" Jesus replied: "**'Love the Lord your God with all your heart and with all your soul and with all your mind.**' This is the first and greatest commandment. And the second is like it: **'Love your neighbor as yourself.**' All the Law and the Prophets hang on these two commandments" (Matt 22:34-40, emphasis mine)

The two Greatest Commandments summarize Christianity, what Christ-followers are expected to pursue and are found in all three synoptic Gospels (Matt 22:34–40; Mark 12:28-33; Luke 10:25-28). Further, Luke's parable of the "Good Samaritan" (10:29-37) shows how all believers need to treat others, as well as many other related lessons (e.g., helping others can be costly, and anyone can be our neighbor). John's Gospel and letters echo this same emphasis on *agape* love. Jesus said that his followers would be known by their love for one another (John 13:35).

In plain language, "God is love" (1 John 4:8, 16). Some segments of Christianity end up inadvertently disobeying the last part of the Great Commission by not teaching responsiveness to the Greatest Commandments. Instead of making disciples who follow Jesus (by learning to obey all he commanded), they end up just making converts. While the first part (transition from unbelief to belief) remains essential, if those same churches ignore the last and more important part (learning how to follow Jesus), those converts may never make the transition to disciples.

Taken together, these comprehensive two mandates of vertical and horizontal love encapsulate the Decalogue. Jesus said that he did not come "to abolish the Law or the Prophets," but to fulfill them (Matt 5:17). The Lamb of God was the perfect sacrifice (Heb 10:14), which rendered the law of sin and death powerless (Rom 8:1-3). In its place, *agape* love forms the foundation of the new covenant which is why the two Greatest Commandments matter.

While all three synoptic Gospels contain the phrases "love God" and "love your neighbor," John's gospel stresses *agape* love. Jesus said that his followers would be known by their love for one another (John 13:35) and that loving him means to obey his teachings (John 14:23). He tells his followers to love each other, just as he loved them (John 15:12).

Mere belief is easier than living out sacrificial *agape* love, but a changed life is an essential goal for Christ-followers (John 13:34-35). The lack of such love leads some observers to conclude that the church has failed to show the world the love of Jesus—which is its primary mission.

Paul repeats Christ's command to love your neighbor (Rom 13:9b, Gal 5:14), and also explains this gospel message in a famous passage from 1 Corinthians chapter 13:1-7. Love never fails.

Both Paul (Gal 5:22-23) and Peter (2 Pet 1:5-11) include love in their lists of spiritual fruit and developmental qualities that echo the words of Jesus. If somehow church leaders miss the foundational role of *agape* love in Christ's teachings, they misconstrue his entire ministry.

WHY THE TWO GREATEST COMMANDMENTS STILL MATTER

The Great Commission indirectly contains the two Greatest Commandments which summarize all that Jesus taught. All four Gospels include text about how Jesus chose the Twelve. They were told to follow, and they responded by becoming his disciples. This was how students followed rabbis at that time. Like a master carpenter apprenticed his successors, rabbis instructed their students. Jesus taught his inner circle with an internship that would enable them to later continue what he had begun because they had been at the feet of their master. Jesus spent about three years with his apostles teaching them about the Greatest Commandments before he gave them the Great Commission. But there was still much his disciples did not understand. Later, Jesus "opened their minds, so they could understand" the things they did not understand while he was with them (Luke 24:44-47).

Jesus said his followers would be known by their love (John 13:34-35). Unfortunately, surveys by the Barna Group, and the Pew Research Center show that American Christianity is not known for its love. In 2007, the Barna Group reported that millions of young people described Christianity as "hypocritical, judgmental, too political, and out of touch with reality." One media commentator's mother told her that, "Christianity used to be more about changing yourself and serving others, but has now become more about changing others and serving yourself." That may be why more recent trends from religious surveys continue to show that a larger percentage of young people claim no religious affiliation when compared to earlier generations.

Surveys are not gospel, of course, but they should cause believers to reflect. This world needs to see more people living like Jesus in their daily lives rather than promoting Jesus with words. Because so many are selling many different products, services, and ideas, unbelievers who see Christlike believers characterized by *agape* love just might notice and ask why they are different (1 Pet 3:15). Regardless of whether others respond, we are called to be faithful rather than successful as the world sees success.

Institutional strategies that neglect the two Greatest Commandments have partly led to today's loveless churchianity. The long-term results of such an approach dishonor rather than glorify God. For those who hear the words of Jesus, but do not put them into practice, the Son of Man called such an approach "building on sand" (Matt 7:21-29)—and that will matter at Judgment.

Rather than continuing to overemphasize the first part of the Great Commission, evangelical leaders should help their existing members become more mature disciples by teaching them to obey all that Jesus commanded, including the two Greatest Commandments.

New believers need to cultivate an "obedience that comes from faith" (Rom 1:5). They need to become more like Christ (1 Cor 11:1), which involves ongoing transformation (Rom 12:2).

Maturity is not likely to develop without help from more seasoned believers to teach new converts. Temptations will occur for every believer (1 Cor 10:13). Even Paul struggled (Rom 7:15). If the immature only learn by trial and error, that is an unforgiving approach with consequences.

Love-based good works done in the name of Christ will honor God. Humble servants glorify their Lord and Master by how they live. Rather than seeking their own reward or recognition, such disciples merely respond as unworthy servants (Luke 17:10).

Attitudes and actions speak much louder than words. Why would anyone seriously consider joining a religion whose main body of believers does not even try to practice the basics that its founder so clearly preached? While no believer will follow Jesus perfectly, if that is not even each believer's spiritual goal, then, of course, they will likely not even begin to resemble their Lord and Master.

MOVING FORWARD

Evangelism is not a higher priority than love. Why? Because evangelism must flow from our love of God and our love of others. Consider Paul's famous passage about the ultimate importance of love, compared to anything else we might do in service of God (1 Cor 13:1-8a).

While Christians are supposed to be different from the world, that has been increasingly called into question. Many churchgoers do not impress others as being anything like Jesus. Being Christ-like embodies God's teachings so that others can see it in practice, so then they might ask about the hope that lies within (1 Pet 3:15). Rather than needing more churchgoers, the world needs more Christ-followers striving, with God's help, to become more like Jesus.

The parable of the Sower (Matt 13:3-23) explains how various factors keep the word of God (the seed) from growing. Lessons about crop failure remain timeless for those who would shepherd and nourish souls. Without learning, applying, and practicing what Jesus taught, the tender new faith-roots of a babe in Christ might never tap into the deeper spiritual truths Jesus taught and modeled for believers to follow.

Spiritual casualties cannot be avoided, but like preventable crop failures, church leaders should do their best to address predictable problems. Many religious institutions have substantial financial assets that will allow them to continue, even with shrinking membership. But the core question remains: "When the Son of Man comes, will he find faith on the earth?" (Luke 18:8b).

From a sociological standpoint, the lack of Christlike love in a nominally religious nation has contributed to the breakdown of the American family. The absence of *agape* love has contributed to materialism, racism, narcissism, and other ungodly cultural realities. Rather than blame culture for its impact on the church, the church needs to accept that it has failed to fulfill its core mission: to teach its converts how to live and love like Jesus. As a result, America's churchgoers have gradually relinquished society to many who completely reject any consideration of God.

10.
The Seduction of Partisan Politics

Partisan politics can easily contaminate, distort, or damage any believer's spirituality.

Exploring how believers can be distracted from following Jesus as Lord and Master has been this book's main goal. No such overview can be complete without touching on partisan politics, and Scripture should set the context for each believer's response to the lure of the temptations it presents. But first, let me cite Lord Acton's famous phrase, "Power tends to corrupt, and absolute power corrupts absolutely." Remember, the original context of this widely used saying resulted from its author's 19th century observations about papal fallibility after the First Vatican Council.

BIBLICAL DISCUSSIONS OF POWER

The term "power" is an ability to make things happen or not happen. God had power as creator (Gen 1:1). As co-creator Jesus also had power (John 1:1-3), but came to earth to serve (Phil 2:5-8). God's son humbled himself when he washed his disciples' feet (John 13:12-18). Paul had a large role in the early church, but saw himself as a servant, as a slave, submissive and loyal to his Lord and Master. Following Jesus does not require power, but focuses upon serving others.

Satan tempted Jesus who had fasted 40 days in the wilderness (Luke 4:1-13). After rejecting the Devil's three propositions, God's son quoted Scripture. When offered power over all the kingdoms on earth in exchange for bowing down to the Devil, Jesus said, "Away from me, Satan! For it is written: 'Worship the Lord your God, and serve him only'" (Matt 4:8-10). Those who follow Jesus are called to resist similar temptations. Partisan politics can easily be viewed as an offer of earthly power. Keep in mind the Devil's strategy. Luke says that the Tempter, "left him until an opportune time" (v. 13). Believers should be aware of such satanic tactics.

The New Testament includes examples of men who sought power for personal use. After seeing that the apostles could impart the Holy Spirit by the laying on of hands, Simon wanted to purchase that power for his own use (Acts 8:18-22). Peter's response to Simon included strong words: "May your silver perish with you," "your heart is not right before God," and you are "captive to sin." John's third letter mentions how Diotrephes "loves to be first," rather than placing God first. Luke records Paul saying that some Ephesian elders would misuse their influence and "distort the truth in order to draw away disciples after them" (Acts 20:30).

Jesus said his kingdom was "not of this world" (John 18:36), a new concept compared to ancient Israel, a theo-political country that combined church and state. As emphasized in the Great Commission (Matt 28:19), the apostles were to make disciples from all ethnic groups, thus expanding God's kingdom to all peoples, not just the twelve tribes that comprised Israel.

Some believers today still harken back to the theo-political context of ancient Israel as their pretext for being active in partisan politics (2 Chr 7:14). But such an approach ignores Jesus, who established a new covenant foretold in the Hebrew Bible. The Sermon on the Mount, for example, contains several phrases discussing "you have heard it said" with how Jesus understands those phrases—their real intent. The book of Hebrews extensively discusses the comparison between old and new covenants.

Ignoring Christian theology, the Constantinian shift combined church and state. Christendom continued such commingling which extended to the founding of America. Many of the original 13 colonies, for example, had explicit provisions requiring that their public officials be Christian (members of their established church). But that is U.S. history, not biblical authorization.

For Christians, the kingdom of God must come first (Matt 6:33) before their secular government. Since believers are "citizens of heaven" (Phil 3:20), they are resident aliens in society. That dual citizenship can create church-state conflicts which will be explored later in this chapter's discussions of political liberty and religious freedom, concepts separate from partisan politics.

Partisan activism typically demands loyalty, while anything that takes the place of allegiance to God is idolatry. Throughout the Hebrew Bible and the New Testament, Scripture condemns other gods. When church leaders divert their followers from prioritizing obedience to all that Jesus commanded, they abuse the power of their position. Believers enmeshed in partisan politics often fail to realize how far they wander from God. Power's subtle temptations can corrupt anyone, especially if they do not have someone close to help them see the potential dangers involved.

WHAT THE NEW TESTAMENT SAYS ABOUT GOVERNMENT

During the time of Christ, Rome governed Israel, but Jesus did not come to establish a theocracy. This was a stumbling block for some Jews who wanted their Messiah to re-establish an earthly kingdom such as the one ruled over by King David. Even after God's son had been resurrected, some disciples still did not understand the difference between Judaism's theocracy and the focus of this new faith on all people everywhere. They asked Jesus if he was "going to restore the kingdom to Israel" (Act 1:6).

During his ministry, some Pharisees publicly tried to entrap Jesus. "What is your opinion?" they asked. "Is it right to pay the imperial tax to Caesar or not?" Instead of directly answering their trick question, Jesus asked to see a coin. He pointed out Caesar's likeness and inscription on the coin as the reason to give Caesar what was his and to God what was his (Matt 22:15-22). That reply touched on the nature of dual, secular-spiritual citizenship, a complex subject all its own.

Paul encourages believers to submit to government whose authority has been granted by God (Rom 13:1-6). That does not mean that all rulers are godly. Paul also urges prayers for those in power (1 Tim 2:1-3) and directs people to obey their rulers and authorities (Titus 3:1). These three passages show a consistency across Paul's writings. Peter's sentiments echoed Paul when he writes, "Love the family of believers, fear God, honor the emperor" (1 Pet 2:13-17).

If government requires sincere believers to do something that conflicts with their personal religious beliefs, they may feel compelled to "obey God rather than man" (Acts 5:29). One past example of such behavior has been conscientious objectors who did not feel they could kill others during war. This chapter's segment on religious freedom discusses related issues.

AMERICA'S CHURCH-STATE BACKGROUND

Christ-followers need reliable background about church-state issues at a time when secular culture warriors increasingly confront people of faith who practice their beliefs in public. America's background is like no other, merits close attention, and greatly matters when discussing the basics of today's partisan politics, political liberty, or religious freedom.

Christianity has greatly influenced culture and politics throughout U.S. history, especially during colonial times. Because of common misrepresentations about this country's origins, I strongly recommend two books that extensively discuss source documents as the basis for their conclusions: *Did America Have A Christian Founding? Separating Modern Myth from Historical Truth*, by Mark David Hall (Nashville: Nelson, 2019); and *Thomas Jefferson and the Wall of Separation Between Church and State*, by Daniel L. Dreisbach (New York: NYU Press, 2002).

When our Revolutionary War broke out, 9 of the 13 colonies had established churches that were supported by taxes. Thus, where colonies had an official religion, Church and State overlapped. In such colonies, religious freedom did not exist because adherents of minority faiths could be prosecuted under civil law. After independence, new state constitutions gradually replaced earlier colonial provisions. Over time, states with established churches eliminated them.

As religious freedom spread, so that no church dictated religion to all its citizens, church leaders remained quite active in politics. Reviewing U.S. history shows that since its beginning, political speeches have contained biblical references. More recent political activism included the Social Gospel movement around the turn of the 20th century and later support for Prohibition (1920-1933). But after adverse publicity about the 1925 Scopes Trial regarding Darwin's theory of evolution, many churches shied away from any political involvement for decades.

During the civil rights struggle of the 1960s, many Black churches pushed for an end to segregation; most white church leaders stayed on the sidelines. After the Moral Majority helped elect President Reagan in 1980, more church leaders and followers became politically active.

BASICS OF PARTISAN POLITICS

The point of America's partisan politics is to win elections for a particular party which then acquires and exercises governmental power to further its purposes. To achieve that result, politicians court religious leaders who can deliver voters to support their party at the ballot box.

America's political climate has changed from bipartisan debate and problem-solving to ideological combat. Almost anything goes, including various "dirty tricks," which have no place in ethical spirituality, but "all's fair in love and war" and politics has become warlike. Each opponent becomes an enemy who must be attacked without mercy, and at every opportunity.

Like many complex topics, of course, there are at least two sides to America's partisan politics. The official side of political parties is expressed in their policy platforms adopted for the record. Later, once in national power, the record of what they accomplish while they have control of the House, Senate, and Presidency, can be compared to campaign promises and official platforms. Some partisan constituencies benefit more than others and how that happens is often masked by legislative details that defy understanding except by experts. The basic rule, practiced by both major parties, is that politicians predictably reward their friends and punish their enemies, either directly or indirectly.

Religious leaders or churchgoers considering partisan activism will face two cultural realities: 1) increased polarization between the political left and right; and 2) hypersensitivity to anyone who questions a particular viewpoint. Satan uses various tactics to entice believers. Grappling with such issues without compromising one's own spiritual foundation requires extreme focus. In her 2017 book, *The Evangelicals, The Struggle to Shape America*, Pulitzer Prize-winning author Frances FitzGerald describes several instances of questionable behavior by prominent church leaders. Rather than mention specific names, I leave the inquisitive to do their own research.

Partisan Politics Conflict with Spirituality

Several aspects of partisan politics can impair any believer's spirituality. Jesus told his followers that they cannot serve two masters, they must choose between God and money (Matt 6:24). Likewise, partisan believers can be torn between pursuing spirituality or party activism. High-profile politicians and political parties demand loyalty, but Jesus calls believers to take up their cross and follow him, the ultimate loyalty. Effort devoted to candidates or issues diverts time away from spiritual goals to a secular agenda that often masquerades as having godly values.

The corrupting influences on those seeking power (candidates) or wielding power (elected officials) might be gauged by examining Paul's characteristics "of a sinful nature" (Gal 5:19-21). Ungodly qualities like hatred, discord, jealousy, selfish ambition, and envy seem all too frequent among those heavily engaged in partisan politics. How often do those seeking or wielding power exhibit "love, joy, peace, patience, kindness, goodness, faithfulness, gentleness, and self-control" (Gal 5:22-23)? As ambassadors for Christ (2 Cor 5:20), believers need to be cautious (Rom 12:18) and careful (Col 4:5-6) with their lives. Peter's building blocks of faith similarly call for believers to add to their faith: goodness, knowledge, self-control, perseverance, godliness, brotherly kindness, and love (2 Pet 1:5-7). He also explains why:

> For if you possess these qualities in increasing measure, they will keep you from being ineffective and unproductive in your knowledge of our Lord Jesus Christ. But if anyone does not have them, he is nearsighted and blind, and has forgotten that he has been cleansed from his past sins. 2 Peter 1:8-9

While not an accurate translation, the late theologian Huston Smith (1919-2016) rephrases the last part of the Lord's Prayer (Matt 6:9-13) in a meaningful way for those overwhelmed with the choices of modern life. Smith suggests in *The Soul of Christianity* that instead of "lead us not into temptation," it should read, "lead us not into confusion or mistaken priorities." Knowing about the various structures of governmental power, I am often tempted to enter the political arena. Whenever I do that, I spend less time trying to follow Jesus because I have been diverted. Thus, I find Smith's above wording to be very helpful to me and might also be helpful to others amid today's complex roles and responsibilities competing for each believer's time.

While some think that believers gifted for potential public service as elected officials should pursue that occupation, I disagree. The knowledge, skills, and abilities that would make for a charismatic politician are also those that would benefit the church, but for spiritual—not secular —purposes. History has shown that poor leadership has hampered many religious organizations. It does benefit society, of course, when people with faith-based ethics serve in various jobs, including government's civil service at any level. But, making the move between any profession and the partisan political arena by seeking or holding elected office involves trade-offs and temptations not otherwise encountered.

Bringing political topics into church discussions can distract from any spiritual climate. Even the smallest issue can create conflict leading to division when Scripture outlines God's desire for unity (John 17:20-23, 1 Cor 1:10-13). Partisan politics inevitably generates tension between different views. So-called wedge issues have been carefully crafted to be exploited by political strategists. Such hot button topics often induce either active support or opposition. When emotional discussions emerge, many churchgoers feel compelled to keep quiet rather than risk expressing a conflicting view. Secular matters can thus easily side-track spiritual pursuits.

Believers need to draw closer to God in all that they do (Jas 4:8). Those who claim Jesus as their

Lord and Master should keep their eyes on "the author and perfecter" of their faith (Heb 12:2). To prevent division, one church near our nation's capital has an unwritten rule to avoid partisan topics.

Twelve Step programs, which profess a higher power, also have Twelve Traditions. Tradition #10 is to avoid controversial outside issues—and instead concentrate on their program's priority.

Modern social media offers ample temptations for anyone to attack those who disagree with them on almost anything. But how does such heated interaction on political topics serve God (Rom 12:18)?

Jesus taught that the true leader is one who serves (Mark 9:35). Following Jesus is not about furthering a personal agenda which is often what American politics involves. On the contrary, becoming more like Jesus requires just the opposite: surrendering personal power.

"Not my will, but yours be done," was Christ's attitude about his heavenly father (Luke 22:42). How can some believers miss that message? Only by focusing on Jesus can we keep ourselves from "being polluted by the world" (Jas 1:27) which includes temptations from partisan politics.

POLITICAL LIBERTY: TRYING TO SHAPE PUBLIC POLICY

While everyone has the individual right to try to influence public policy, people soon learn that they can exert more influence in groups organized around common principles. In America, that is their political liberty because the Declaration of Independence includes the phrase: "life, liberty, and the pursuit of happiness." Thus, every group, including religious ones, has the option of trying to shape public policy, but how that happens has changed over time.

At the founding of this country, an exercise of political liberty led to the Bill of Rights. Those unhappy with God not being mentioned in the Constitution insisted on an amendment that would constrain the new national government. Remember, when ratified, the First Amendment did not apply to the states, which jealously guarded their prerogatives. Founders guarded against a strong central authority like one they had just fought against for their independence. But beginning after the Civil War's 14th Amendment and at the turn of the 20th century, the Supreme Court gradually applied constitutional guarantees to all states. This emerging federalism clarified the division of roles and responsibilities between our national government and each state. For example, each state regulates its own elections and criminal law (if there is no conflict with federal law), but constitutional interpretations determine federal rights, including religious freedom.

While some use the terms religious liberty and religious freedom interchangeably, I find that confusing. Instead, I link the term liberty to the Declaration and the term freedom to the Constitution.

Explained in the next segment, religious freedom protects those trying to practice their faith, but does not try to shape public policy which is the point of political liberty.

When church leaders encourage their followers to exercise their political liberty, it can take away from their efforts to help their churchgoers follow Jesus and should normally be discouraged. Exceptions exist, but must be carefully considered. How often does God need human help?

As the country moves further away from historical traditions, anything religious has come under increasing attack. Many antitheists want to eliminate religion from the public square, and exile faith to private spaces. They object to any vestiges of even the civil religion that has historically shaped this country, such as "In God We Trust" on our money, or "under God" in our Pledge of Allegiance, or "so help me God" in any oath. In response to such attacks on public faith, the strong temptation for many religious people has been to exercise their political liberty by taking certain battles to the public policy arena—but that has social costs. Pollsters report that many now negatively view Christianity partly because of partisan activism by high-profile religious leaders. That is, of course, not how Jesus said his followers would be known (John 14:35).

If there is no clear religious purpose to partisan activism or political involvement, why should church leaders and followers devote themselves to secular causes instead of Jesus? Trying to make public policy conform to religious morality, for example, creates secular opposition. Further, it would not convert an unbeliever to a believer by forcing them to obey religiously themed laws. When the Roman government required unbelievers to convert or perish, what resulted did not make them into Christians, but merely made them churchgoers. Spiritual relationships cannot be forced, and perceived persecution logically creates resentment.

Secular laws adopted to mirror godly morality would not establish a relationship with God. While one of Scripture's purposes is to convince unbelievers to convert, the apostle Paul wrote that God's guidance is for those who believe, not for those who do not (1 Cor 5:9-13).

In any case, voting remains the primary way for people to shape government policies. When choosing among candidates, character has always been a factor, not just someone's religious views. But when church leaders advocate for a particular candidate (despite IRS prohibitions), they squander their scarce persuasive power for secular, not spiritual, purposes. Rather, helping their followers to become more like Jesus should be each spiritual leader's primary motivation as they continue to guide each member of their flock toward growth "in Christ."

RELIGIOUS FREEDOM: OBEYING GOD
RATHER THAN MEN

America's religious freedom depends upon how our Supreme Court interprets the Constitution:

> "Congress shall make no law respecting an **establishment** of religion, or prohibiting the **free exercise** thereof; or abridging the freedom of speech, or of the press; or the right of the people peaceably to assemble, and to petition the Government for a redress of grievances." First Amendment, adopted in 1791, (emphasis mine).

For perspective, it is often overlooked that this nation quickly affirmed the role of religion in public life, even before the First Amendment became law. Previously enacted under the Articles of Confederation, the Continental Congress passed the Northwest Ordinance of 1787 which in part states: "Religion, Morality and knowledge being necessary to good government and the happiness of mankind, Schools and the means of education shall be forever encouraged."

The establishment clause prevents the nation from favoring one religion over another. The free exercise clause means that the federal government would not interfere with the practice of religion. Though religion has arguably lost its dominant role in America, our Constitution still protects its free exercise from being limited by those who object to any public expression of faith. Those who defend their religious freedom in court are not trying to force their religious beliefs on others, but are fighting to live their lives according to how they view God's guidance.

As antitheists increasingly organize to oppose religion, more churches and churchgoers may find themselves in a defensive posture, battling to avoid government interference in how they practice their faith. Some recent constitutional clashes pit the rights of various groups against certain faith-based concepts, which is permissible in our pluralistic democracy. But by the same token, believers with strong convictions object to being silenced for their religious views.

For biblical perspective, early in the apostolic era, the Sanhedrin confronted Peter and those with him and told them not to teach about Jesus. In reply, they said, "We must obey God rather than men!" (Acts 5:29). They expressed obedience to a higher power: God, not men. In much the same way, those who practice their religion today and depend on their constitutional rights to protect them, respond to a higher authority than human law: their allegiance to a heavenly father.

MOVING FORWARD

Rather than exercise their political liberty to change government, a better way for churchgoers to improve America is to become more like Jesus. Authentic disciples will become even more counter-cultural than ever by allowing the two Greatest Commandments to reshape their lives. But, amid increasing attacks on anyone demonstrating faith-based morality, some believers who just want to be left alone to practice their faith will have to defend themselves in court.

Meanwhile, something as basic as churchgoers obeying the last six of the Ten Commandments—how to treat others—would enrich this country. Many socio-economic injustices would be lessened if more churchgoers treated their neighbors according to the Golden Rule. In a nominally Christian nation, few of its citizens respect God's directions that, if followed, would reduce materialism, racism, narcissism, and many other problems that plague our culture. Some churches have allowed their members to go on living like everyone else and calling themselves Christians when they may not have even been trying to become more like Jesus. If only church leaders showed more concern for each member's spiritual status and growth, maybe many more churchgoers might live their daily lives in pursuit of God's agenda, not their own.

It is not possible to intelligently discuss partisan activism without considering how it impacts spiritual development. The subtle trade-offs that invariably occur can become an obstacle to living one's faith. When party loyalty is valued over everything else, believers have taken their eyes off Jesus.

God's son beckons his followers to take up their crosses, not enter the political arena. Further, political opponents often attack. When Christ-followers find themselves being persecuted, it should be for godly living (2 Tim 3:12), not their political stances.

Consider adding another comparison to Paul's words: "There is neither Jew nor Greek, slave nor free, male nor female, (Democrat nor Republican) for you are all one in Christ Jesus." (Gal 3:28). When written, it would have been difficult to describe a greater contrast than between those three biblical groupings. While party affiliations may not be fully comparable to the scriptural contrasts in this passage, they are at least understandable. What should matter most to those who follow Jesus is their unity of spiritual purpose as they each take up their own cross and serve only God as best they can.

11.
Following Jesus, No Matter What

Following Jesus is a life-long commitment, not a one-time conversion event.

When I was hired to be a Program Budget Analyst in Alaska's OMB, part of my informal orientation included this memorable advice: we must all become our own general manager. In the final analysis, each of us is responsible for our own career decisions, for working toward our own goals. While we can blame others for some things, most of our lives depend on our own decisions or sometimes our failure to decide. However, once we know where we are headed, we can seek help, but we cannot expect others to make the key choices that shape our existence. Our faith depends on similar factors based on the choices we each make and continue to make throughout life.

Each believer's relationship with God starts when they initially respond at conversion, but their continued growth greatly influences their ability to serve. Nobody but you can navigate the complex dynamics involved in assessing and implementing the right combination of belief and practice. The ongoing need to balance orthodoxy and orthopraxy will shape how well you transition from mere churchgoer to a Christ-follower who grows as God intends. As Jesus promised, the Holy Spirit helps each believer doing their best to serve their Lord and Master.

"Following Jesus, no matter what" requires that each believer realize that life's challenges will severely test your faith in God and thus require periodic rededication to strengthen resolve.

DISCIPLES NEED SELF-DISCIPLINE

The vertical aspect of faith (loving God) and the horizontal aspect of faith (loving others) will involve more than just periodic gatherings with large groups of other believers. How each believer manages that remains a personal challenge, subject to their own spiritual self-discipline.

In his 1946 classic, *Man's Search for Meaning*, Viktor Frankl explored the darkest side of WWII's Nazi Germany. He survived the Auschwitz death camp to write much more than his own survival story. Frankl evaluated how some people managed to endure the worst imaginable circumstances. His answer? Having a "purpose beyond self" kept many alive when others, who saw no meaning in their suffering, just gave up. Frankl also notes two other core motivations: pleasure and power. Today, we are all shaped by one or more of these three.

Most choose pleasure. Some choose power. Few choose the purpose beyond self of a sacrificial life.

Instead of a purpose beyond self, today's American culture seems primarily focused on self. The concept of taking and posting on-line images of oneself has pervaded our culture. Media followers translate to personal revenue. When it comes to opinions about almost anything, amateurs elevate the importance of their own views above professionals with credentials. Few willingly accept submission to any type of authority figure. But those who follow Jesus must make a countercultural commitment to serve God rather than to lead a self-centered life.

HOW AM I SUPPOSED TO FOLLOW JESUS IF LEADERS DO NOT HELP?

How does one follow Jesus? Your congregation, with all its good intentions, may not be inclined or equipped to do that. Still, your church's main goal should be to teach you basics and then to help you grow, to teach you discipleship, to help you follow Jesus. But as we have seen in previous chapters, churches tend to look out for their own institutional interests. If your church is not helping you become more like Jesus, you must prayerfully evaluate your spiritual situation.

It may be that you decide to seek a body of believers that pays attention to the spiritual maturity of its members. If you are unable or disinclined to find such a group, you will need to make some adjustments where you are. Try to connect with the kind of people who remind you of Jesus.

Do not assume the person who helps you will be on staff at your church or in a position of formal leadership. But do not assume the opposite, either. Many who have chosen a life in ministry are sincere in their pursuit of helping others follow Christ. You might be able to thrive because of your leaders, not despite them. Still, it is important that you pay close attention to the depth of your spiritual life, because for better or worse those around you help shape your progress.

God First

As you are looking for someone to guide you, remember the first Greatest Commandment. Start by deepening your relationship with God. Actively pursue spiritual disciplines like meditation, study, and maybe even fasting especially if that would be a new exercise in devotion. Refocus your life toward spiritual pursuits. This is a lifelong process that requires courageous choices and prayerfully considered actions (see Chapter 8, "Loving God," concerning vertical theology).

Do not put too many expectations on the speed of your growth as you practice a pattern of discipline. God does not work on human timelines. Sometimes transformation happens quickly. Other times it happens slowly, like a seed that gradually grows from a sapling into a mighty tree.

Be patient with yourself. Just as conversion from unbelief to belief required changes, so will the transition from churchgoer to Christ-follower. Periodically reassess your direction, where you have been, and where you are headed. Success includes gradual progress toward a worthy goal. Remember, God did not guarantee life to be free of temptation, trials, or tribulations.

Ask Around

Sometimes believers get caught up in an institutional allegiance without even knowing it. You will know that you are talking to someone who will not be a good mentor when they grow bewildered or agitated by your focus on Jesus. Your questions or concerns may seem threatening. For many churchgoers, their only response to deeper questions about following Jesus will be to refer you to clergy. Such believers cannot offer you what they do not have themselves.

Those who cannot feed themselves will not be able to help you. Maybe they have never learned how to move beyond their doctrinal beginnings or tried to authentically practice their faith.

Do not be discouraged. Even if some of the people in your church are stagnant, others may be able to help. You may find a depth of discipleship in someone who completely surprises you. Some of the quietest members of any flock may have the richest relationship with Jesus and could be a store of spiritual wisdom waiting to be shared. Finding such followers can begin with a casual conversation to probe whether a particular churchgoer may also be a Christ-follower.

Spiritual Community

If you are not already connected to a spiritual community, you need to look for a healthy church. Find a group that is serious about discipleship, about responding to God, and that holds a high view of Scripture. Does this church depend totally on clergy or are there older, more mature believers, able to teach the less mature? Carefully consider their historic use of small groups.

Look for a church whose leadership cares about the spiritual health of each individual sheep. Do vibrant small groups discuss everything from Sunday's sermon to random topics without fear of being chastised? Look for people who know how to be genuine and open with each other.

Remember, growth takes time. As you become more like Jesus, realize that you will not have everything figured out and never will. But you will need to develop your own personal answers to faith questions that might come up, doing the best you can when asked (1 Pet 3:15).

Satan Remains

After forty days in the wilderness, Satan could not successfully tempt Jesus, but planned to return at a "more opportune time." Believers can rest assured that they also remain targeted by God's ultimate enemy. Our adversary attacks in different ways, some subtle, some direct.

Satan's goal is to divert, distract, or deceive as many as possible. In so doing, the "prince of this world" has a major influence on this life. Those who claim that God micromanages everything in this life according to a plan have some explaining to do when bad things happen that have no clear connection to God's purpose. There is a big difference between God causing bad things to happen, and God helping you make the best of a situation where bad things have already happened.

A CALL TO CHURCHES

Just because it is an individual's responsibility to follow Jesus does not mean church leaders are immune from accountability. If your church is entrenched in how things have always been done, it is past time to reassess what you are doing. Is your main purpose to defend your statement of faith, or to help lead your followers toward becoming more like Jesus, or something else?

What motivations drive your church to do what it does? Is it designed to make the people who have always been attending feel comfortable? Or does it actively try to reach new believers and help them grow into maturing Christ-followers? Or is it something else? You might be amazed at how much your church improves if various parts of your theological body are growing healthier.

If unbelievers with no previous religious affiliation encounter Jesus in your congregation, they might be surprised. Instead of unbiblical tradition, legalism, or something else, they might discover that God's son has much to say that they did not previously understand or appreciate.

There are many tools available to help a church reshape, reframe, and reconsider its future. A mini-reformation will be required for most religious groups to repent of their institutional focus. If groups change their goal from just doing church to becoming the body of Christ, a sanctified people will emerge ready to serve their Lord and Master.

A CALL TO GOD'S PEOPLE

You need to decide if you need help to become more like Jesus. If you cannot find a spiritual mentor, it might be time to look elsewhere. Take your time and consider where you have been. What was your church doing well? What was missing? If you visit elsewhere, do not expect to find the perfect church—it does not exist and never has. But churches that prioritize the spiritual health of their people do exist. Look for one of those. Your spiritual future may depend on it.

Assess your own spiritual toolkit; how many talents do you have to serve God? How have they been used? Have you internalized Scripture? Babes in Christ wandering around become easy prey. Nature's predators cull out the weak from among a flock and Satan remains a roaring lion.

Remember that where two or three believers are gathered, God remains in their midst, so maybe your answer lies closer than you think. Spiritual challenges offer both danger and opportunity.

It is a mistake to think that following Jesus consists of a list of what to do and what not to do, though that is appropriate to some degree. Rather, it requires relationships. It is a process of becoming more like God's son, and in doing so bringing honor to God by your imperfect efforts to serve your Creator. The great deception of churchianity is its empty promise of salvation.

Concluding Thoughts

What does it mean to follow Jesus? First, it means studying his life—the things he said, the things he did, and the priorities he set. Remember, though, if it was easy to become like Jesus by just deciding what to believe and studying his life, the world would be a more spiritual place. Some churchgoers have become apathetic because of their leaders. Thus, it can be difficult to discern following the real Jesus from following the Jesus painted for us by organized religion. We must continue returning to the source—the Gospels and stories about the early church in Acts. We must humble ourselves, leave misconceptions behind, and spend time with the multi-layered teachings of Jesus. His lessons will become more real as we put them into practice.

Second, following Jesus is a lifelong commitment. When Jesus called his disciples, he did not say, follow me for a little while to that town over there. He said, "Follow me." No destination. No time limit. Just a simple instruction to leave everything else behind. The words of Jesus still echo down the centuries to us. He did not hesitate to use strong language. "If anyone would come after me, he must deny himself and take up his cross daily and follow me" (Luke 9:23).

Third, many come to the end of their lives and have regrets about what they did or did not do. Too many learn, too late, the full cost of their choices and the priorities they followed. The National Football League finally acknowledged the impact of chronic traumatic encephalopathy (CTE). But a confirmed diagnosis requires a post-mortem brain exam. While alive, former NFL players can exhibit several telltale symptoms of CTE, but certainty must wait for an autopsy. Similarly, many churches experience symptoms, but waiting for an institutional autopsy will be too late for the individuals involved, especially for those who depend on their church to save them.

Fourth, this book has painted a limited, diagnostic picture for struggling believers to consider; what comes next will always be an individual choice. God offers everyone a chance to be adopted into an eternal family, but such a placement still requires acceptance and response.

Fifth, with God, it is not about our personal perfection, but rather our long-term direction as reflected in our life's choices. A cousin repeated an old saying she found to be true: "Not all the Christians are in church, and not all those in church are Christian." Will you be judged to be merely a churchgoer who claims to know Jesus, or will you be acknowledged by Jesus as one of his followers who did their best to put into practice his words, who built upon the ultimate rock?

Finally, the following passages offer encouragement:

"Do not let your hearts be troubled. Trust in God; trust also in me. In my Father's house are many rooms; if it were not so, I would have told you. I am going there to prepare a place for you. And if I go and prepare a place for you, I will come back and take you to be with me that you also may be where I am. (John 14:1-4)

And we pray this in order that you may live a life worthy of the Lord and may please him in every way: bearing fruit in every good work, growing in the knowledge of God, being strengthened with all power according to his glorious might so that you may have great endurance and patience, and joyfully giving thanks to the Father, who has qualified you to share in the inheritance of the saints in the kingdom of light. For he has rescued us from the dominion of darkness and brought us into the kingdom of the Son he loves, in whom we have redemption, the forgiveness of sins. (Col 1:10-14)

For those who like to focus on only one thought, in the Beatitudes, Jesus assures us that those who "hunger and thirst for righteousness" will be filled (Matt 5:6).

Epilogue

While questioning institutions that many hold dear, my intent has been to glorify God by helping individual believers, who may be on the verge of wandering away from faith, to rededicate themselves. Some churchgoers may not realize how far they have strayed in their mind without having physically left. Modern Christianity needs to refocus upon teaching churchgoers how to follow Jesus and constantly confront God's enemy: Satan. That ecumenical lesson applies to the church universal, to each congregation, and, of course, to each believer

Any church that claims to be Christian should help its members learn how to respond to Jesus, who beckoned with the original invitation to "follow me." Unless those who claim his name make Jesus their life's priority, they will not do well when God's son returns (Matt 7:21-29).

One of my biggest concerns is for those who think they are headed to heaven because they believe in their church rather than in following Jesus (as if their conversion from unbelief or joining a church guarantees them eternity). Such an approach that emphasizes only the right "salvation protocol" (what must I do to be saved) sells God's kingdom as a membership, rather than a lifetime journey.

Those who see Jesus as just a Savior need to know him and be known by him. Otherwise, they are missing the meaning of what it means to try to become more like him. If you or your church get the basics of Christianity wrong, then you misunderstand Christ.

All readers should ponder what they need to do next, where they need to go. I offer no short-cuts to next-level spirituality, but only suggestions. The rest is up to you; "Test everything. Hold on to the good" (1 Thes 5:21). May our heavenly Father and his Holy Spirit guide you through life as you become more like Jesus.

Maranatha! (1 Cor 16:22b)

Acknowledgements

Like many writers, I have adopted much from others. When there is a reference to the work of an author, I cited the source. But I have also noted unattributed thoughts within quotation marks so that readers will know when I am using someone else's words or phrases which are not my own. Further, Chapter 6, "Loving God" was drafted by one of my editors who prefers to remain anonymous, a choice I respect.

This project has taken years, so I would be remiss if I did not acknowledge that I stand on the shoulders of giants, especially the late Dallas Willard. His own book, *The Great Omission*, influenced me so much, I borrowed his title for my chapter 9.

As with any book, many contributed, but I am reluctant to credit any except those whose works are cited because I am critical of many church practices. In return for critiquing many sacred traditions, I expect many of my views to be questioned, rejected, or even militantly countered. When privately discussing my title in a local bookstore, a stranger overheard and berated me for taking issue with Christianity. Other incidents have also targeted me, so I hesitate to put those who helped me in that situation, but they have my appreciation for their substantial contributions.

As usual, any errors or omissions in this book remain my responsibility. Further, no reader should infer and I have not intended to imply that I have achieved any degree of spiritual maturity that I recommend for those seeking to be authentic Christ-followers. Like many, I have fallen short in my personal and professional life, but especially in my roles as an individual churchgoer, a Bible class teacher, and as a church leader. My recurring prayer is that God will use my failures to teach me and help me grow. My hope is that this book includes helpful experiences and lessons I have learned, and some I am still working on, to assist others in their journey to become more like Jesus.

About the Author

If you benefited from this book, please consider posting an online review. Thank you in advance.

*

If you have specific concerns about its contents, you may email the author at mikeclemens907@gmail.com.

After serving his home congregation for over thirty years, Michael J. "Mike" Clemens resigned as an elder and spent the next twenty years on an ill-defined sabbatical, trying to refocus his spiritual life.

This book synthesizes lessons learned from several sources, including 1) academic life where he earned a BA in Economics from Oregon State and a Master of Public Administration from the University of Alaska, Juneau, 2) three years as a Coast Guard Officer, 3) three decades of administrative work with the State of Alaska, and 4) extensive reading about contemporary Christianity.

Married for 55 years, he and his wife have three children, nine grandchildren, and five great-grandchildren. Mike grew up in Portland, Oregon, but has lived in Juneau, Alaska, since being stationed there after graduation from Officer Candidate School in early 1970. Converted from unbelief a few months later, he served the Juneau Church of Christ faithfully in various capacities including the local eldership from October, 1999 until February, 2002 when he resigned. In early 2024, he began reconnecting with that same congregation.

About the Publisher

Sulis International Press publishes select fiction and nonfiction in a variety of genres under four imprints:

- Riversong Books (fiction)

- Sulis Press (general nonfiction)

- Keledei Publications (spirituality)

- Sulis Academic Press (academic works)

For more, visit the website at
https://sulisinternational.com

Subscribe to the newsletter at
https://sulisinternational.com/subscribe/

Follow on social media
https://www.facebook.com/SulisInternational
https://twitter.com/Sulis_Intl
https://www.pinterest.com/Sulis_Intl/
https://www.instagram.com/sulis_international/

Made in the USA
Middletown, DE
11 March 2025